LINESCAPES

LINESCAPES

Remapping and Reconnecting Britain's
Fragmented Wildlife

HUGH WARWICK

◨ SQUARE PEG

10 9 8 7 6 5 4 3 2 1

Square Peg, an imprint of Vintage,
20 Vauxhall Bridge Road,
London SW1V 2SA

Square Peg is part of the Penguin Random House group of companies
whose addresses can be found at global.penguinrandomhouse.com.

Penguin
Random House
UK

www.vintage-books.co.uk

A CIP catalogue record for this book is available from the British Library

ISBN 9780224100892

Typset in 12.5/17 pt Adobe Garamond by Jouve (UK), Milton Keynes
Printed and bound in Great Britain by Clays Ltd, St Ives Plc

Penguin Random House is committed to a sustainable future
for our business, our readers and our planet. This book is made
from Forest Stewardship Council® certified paper.

MIX
Paper from
responsible sources
FSC
www.fsc.org   FSC® C018179

To Zoe, Mati and Pip – who keep me connected

CONTENTS

Introduction   1

1 Archaeological Lines   13
2 Hedges   28
3 Ditches and Dykes   58
4 Walls   79
5 Ancient Paths and Green Lanes   102
6 Canals   123
7 Railways   150
8 Roads   175
9 Pylons and Pipelines   204
10 Unfragmentation   221
11 Reconnection   243

Notes   249
Acknowledgements   253
Index   255

INTRODUCTION

Sitting by the window in a cramped and crowded train as it bundled through undulating Lancashire fields on a July afternoon, I paused from trying to read, to gaze outside. Sunshine was vying with clouds to set up an ominous contrast, but in places it broke through to shine spotlights onto the landscape.

When I had last paid attention we had been lurching towards Wolverhampton between parallel lines. On one side of us, the Birmingham Canal, uninviting and unloved, dark water sitting in a stream of concrete. On the other, the M5, dystopian brutalism at its finest, stagnant too, the stream of vehicles static.

Now, out in the countryside, very different lines were visible. Beyond the blurred verge, parallax slowed the middle distance to a sedentary stroll, giving me time to see more: hedges, some rich and vibrant, wandering through fields worn thin by livestock. Walls, inanimate minerals come to life and hinting of hidden depths.

There was a connection between these two different views. I was struck, yet again, by how linear most man-made features in the landscape were. When we set about the land for ownership and control, we tend to do so with lines.

Let us shift perspective. When my son was six he was given the opportunity by his grandfather to fly a light aircraft. Pip sat in a car seat so he could see out of the cockpit; I was in the back, utterly terrified, as my father-in-law took his hands off the controls and told my son to have a go. Looking out of the window to distract myself I was presented with a view of the Cambridgeshire countryside from 1,000 feet up. The threads that cut it up and tied it together were stark: road, rail and canal links – but also hedgerows, tree lines, woodlands. You could also see how much communities – the clusters of brown buildings that represented villages, towns, estates – had been carved up, divided by all these lines. As our lives were being threaded together by the lines we made, so at the same time the landscape was being sliced into ever-smaller fragments. I struggled to find a straight line made by nature.

It is rare to discover a view of the landscape untouched by our lines. So dominant a feature have they become that they have transformed our landscape into something new. As urban living has created the cityscape, so our lines have created what I call a linescape; one where the lines we have drawn have far-reaching consequences.

We use these lines for connection, and we use them for separation. It is a paradox that the very first lines we etched into the land were specifically for fragmentation: walls, hedges, ditches and dykes, all there to assert ownership or restrain livestock – yet inadvertently they have become the agents of connection for wildlife. It is along their edges that our flora and fauna thrive and flourish.

The very lines we carved into the landscape for connection, on the other hand – canals, railways and roads – have become agents of fragmentation for wildlife, cutting habitats into ever smaller, and increasingly unviable, pockets.

The dichotomy is not quite so simple, though, as this book will explore. There are hedges that fulfil none of their promise, and roads along which wildlife runs riot. And while I have a prejudice in favour of hedges – for Wordsworth 'little lines of sportive wood run wild' – I want to be challenged. I want to find the good, even in the most unlikely places.

*

My fascination with the world of lines comes from the animal I started to study over thirty years ago. Perhaps more than any other animal, the hedgehog is defined by lines. It is named after the linear feature it 'hogs', and it is famously rendered two-dimensional by the road. Over time I have broadened my vision to encompass other species, and while there are many differences between bees, bats, otters, moths, robins, toads and water voles, I have come to recognise one constant: the impact that the fragmentation of their habitats is having on their ability to flourish.

Fragmentation is an under-reported and poorly understood threat. Most attention is paid to the loss of habitat, and there is no denying how serious a problem this is. In the last seventy years we have lost 97 per cent of wildflower meadows, and 75 per cent of ponds and heaths. Fifty per cent of our ancient woodland has gone in the last one hundred years. But beneath these alarming figures is a further tragedy that should be at the top of the conservation agenda. The remaining pockets of habitat are becoming increasingly isolated.

The problems presented by fragmentation are both immediate and genetic. When there has been a glut of young, for example, an absence of suitable mates or a shortage of food, animals need to move to new habitat. When they are restricted from moving, the risk of localised extinctions increases. Living within restricted habitats has a further impact on the genetic diversity of individual animals and is the subject of current research.

Hedgehogs are a species whose length of leg tends to argue against extensive perambulation, but they have recently been revealed to require far greater areas than previously thought for viable populations. Computer modelling now projects the minimum habitat required for a sustainable population as the size of three 18-hole golf courses. That means just under a square kilometre – and not chopped up by fences, roads or canals. Where are we going to find that?

*

For the successful conservation of species, size really does matter. SLoSS – Single Large or Several Small – is how the question is scientifically phrased: what is going to be the most effective way to assist a species or an ecosystem? One large reserve, or lots of smaller ones? It might seem self-evident that we should always choose 'Single Large' – but ecology, especially when it has to be considered alongside such tedious realities as budgetary constraints, can be a complicated soul. Moreover, for many species – such as the brown hairstreak butterfly or the bank vole – edges are a crucial component of their habitat, and when the areas are smaller the relative amount of edge is greater. So smaller areas have advantages too – but they need to be connected. The answer to the question, then, is not a simple yes/no: yes, we need single large areas, but we need several small ones too. Single large areas can become fragmented as effectively as the small ones can become connected.

This book, therefore, is going to look at how the bad can be made good, and the good, better. Connection is not just important for wildlife: it is a central tenet of what it means to be human – that we crave (or at least most of us do) connection with others of the same species. In fact, a large body of evidence indicates that we long for a connection with other species too.

This 'biophilia', a term popularised by the Harvard University biologist E. O. Wilson, who has done so much to bring an awareness of the need for biodiversity to a wider audience, has serious implications. We need nature, and nature needs us to treat it with greater care. There is an obvious logic to this – if we turn the planet into a barren wasteland, we too will die – but Wilson's thesis is subtler. The need, he argues, is both physiological and psychological. We are happier in nature. We feel better, convalesce faster and learn more deeply, when we have contact with nature.

'We will not fight to save what we do not love.' So said another American biologist and writer, Stephen Jay Gould, in discussing the need to conserve species. Though this principle should, I would argue, be at the heart of the conservation movement, we should not be fooled by the easy lure of the charismatic megafauna – the lions, dolphins, whales and pandas. We are most likely to fall in love with the girl or the boy next door – we need to look for love where we have a chance of finding it, which, for nature, is going to be in the species that are already around us, that we are already, did we but look, connected to, and could be more so. When training people in hedgehog ecology I ask them to 'think hedgehog' – which leads to them lying on the grass to gain a different perspective.

So many measures of biodiversity value are made on the basis of organisms that travel through the air. Insects, birds and bats, obviously, but also plants that have seed that can fly or be flown. We need to measure the wildlife value for the things that creep, crawl and snuffle as much as for the flamboyant and flighty. Connection is at the heart of what we need, and what nature needs, if we are to begin to tackle the global collapse of species and change in climate we have engineered.

The Anthropocene period is upon us: a new epoch identified by the planet-wide impact of human activities. The results for future generations are far from determined. But if we can make and maintain connections, both for and with wildlife, it is just possible we might be able to avert the worst.

'I believe that empathy,' wrote Philosopher Roman Krznaric, '– the imaginative act of stepping into another person's shoes and viewing the world from their perspective – is a radical tool for social change and should be a guiding light for the art of living.'[1] Clearly he is right: without the capacity to imagine the world through other people's lives we lose one of the key elements of humanity. But I believe we should take the idea of empathy further.

The point at which we begin to see our world from the perspective of the living things and communities that inhabit it is the point at which we can truly embark on a revolutionary shift in the way we interact with the world. This does not require great leaps of anthropomorphism. We are not going to need to personalise the world around us: we just need to start looking at it a little differently.

Looking more closely at these man-made lines from the perspective of the wildlife they affect reveals key differences, for example, between the multidimensional space inside a drystone wall compared to the flat tarmac of a motorway; the irony of railway tracks threatened by leaves, compared to the leaves that make up a hedge; the metal-banked canals compared to the moist depths of a ditch. Their natural history, meanwhile, gives unique insight into the wildscape of Great Britain. The earliest lines created by humans were, inevitably, directly related to the underlying geology and ecology of the region in which they emerged. The lichens and mosses that have colonised walls – their splashes of colour and pads of green – speak of the microclimate the walls have created, and also of the rocks from which their stones were originally hewn.

It is a deep history, summarised most accessibly nowadays in Francis Pryor's *The Making of the British Landscape*. The bedrock of Britain is probably around 1 billion years old. That ancient foundation has been subjected to the thrusts and ructions of time, and its recent geology is a result of the last 2.5 million years of ice and weathering, which is in turn reflected in the ecology we see on the surface. So while the north and west of the country leans towards a harder sedimentary and volcanic rock, the south and east tends towards softer and more recent rocks of chalk and limestone. An appreciation of a linescape is deepened, therefore, by being able to see more than the limited vision granted to us by the cartographers. I want us all to look at the linescapes of Britain with new eyes. Because while nature does not tend to straight lines and discrete borders, naturally preferring a meandering indiscretion, our lines can and do contain a real potential for wildness.

*

By now on my train journey to Stirling we were higher up, and somewhere in Cumbria. The train had stopped. Where there had been hedges, now walls asserted their dominance. Brisker life beyond the window, wind whipping up horsetail clouds; but in the shelter of the wall and a small hollow, a cup of yellow in a sea of green; a butter-rich glaze relishing the still damp air.

I returned to my iPad and tried to concentrate again. I was trying to cram as much of one important document before journey's end. A government White Paper may not be the sort of thing to get most people's pulses racing, and I had started with low expectations and high sense of duty. But as I swiped the pages of *Making Space for Nature* delight began to grow, and the conjunction of reading and seeing inspired in me a feeling of excitement and connection. Subtitled 'A Review of England's Wildlife Sites and Ecological Network', it was commissioned by the then Secretary of State for the Department for Environment, Food and Rural Affairs, Hilary Benn, and published in September 2010, and its author, Professor Sir John Lawton, was addressing those in power with authority and passion. He was basing his work on science rather than rhetoric, and pushing for something tangible: a real, nationwide shift in attitudes and relationship to the natural world.

He talked with such optimism, even if in retrospect it seems rather naïve, quoting with approval Hilary Benn's own words: 'Now is the time to see how we can enhance ecological England further. Linking together areas to make ecological corridors and a connected network, could have real benefits in allowing nature to thrive.' That was fighting talk. Sir John called for the formation of what became Nature Improvement Areas, and stated fearlessly that a budget of £1.1 billion a year should be set aside for the conservation of life on planet Britain.

Those big numbers were for someone else to worry about. I was excited by the focus on fragmentation, and more importantly the ways in which connectivity can be woven back into the fabric of our landscape by working with the lines we already have. 'The commitment of the new coalition Government to nature conservation in general,' Sir John himself went on with such enthusiasm, 'and to the promotion of "green corridors" in particular, is heartening.'

If a week is a long time in politics, what are several years? When former Prime Minister David Cameron talked of the 'greenest government ever', some might have raised their hopes for a serious change in the way the country is run. Though when the same person was reported as saying, 'We have got to get rid of all this green crap' it is hard to know what to believe. And now, there is little evidence that the environment is being taken seriously at all.

*

Not all lines are man-made – there are natural lines that can look a little too perfect not to be made by man. Beavers, for example, build dams to create lakes that act as both a food store and a defence against predators, and in flat lands these dams can be hundreds of metres long, and strong enough to carry people (I have walked along the top of beaver-dams). These dams then formed early pathways through boggier landscapes, and were used to link communities in places like the Somerset Levels.

Then there can be those lines of trees just too perfectly aligned not to be man-made. Looking to the uplands, hills and mountains are often tonsured. A perfect ring of trees beneath the bald scalp. Though on closer inspection these lines are far more organic with the trees shrinking and twisting as the elevation increases. The treeline is a rare natural line.

And some of the man-made linescapes we now revere were once contentious. As the 'hedgerow poet' John Clare suffered the ravages of the enclosures, manifested by thousands of miles of new hedges, so some wildlife took up the opportunity to branch out from the restricted range of the woodland edge and take great strides along these newly laid lines. Time travel would let us see how the fragmentation of the landscape caused by the enclosures assisted in their spread. The arrival of hedges – vastly expanding the amount of woodland edge – was perhaps the greatest thing that happened for the hedgehog.

Of course, our lines go back far earlier than the enclosures. When did we first mark the land with lines? The first would have been temporary; barriers to provide some protection from the wild nights – lines seem such a statement of order in the face of the organic chaos of nature. It is not hard to imagine proto-human *Homo erectus* (the most successful hominid, surviving for around a million years, while *Homo sapiens* has only notched up 200,000 years so far) making the first lines as brushwood fences, 1.8 million years ago. Evidence of stick picket, woven and wattle fences has been found dating back more than 600,000 years, while hedged banks and dry-stone walls were first introduced along with arable cultivation more than 10,000 years ago.

It was the Neolithic farmers who etched some of our very first lines into the landscape. Hedges, ditches, dykes, and walls: for most of the last 5,000 years, the lines have been organic; they have allowed nature to wander along our barricades. The gentle expansion of these ways accelerated with the Industrial Revolution into something more aggressive, covering most of the land, cutting ever deeper. Canals, railways, roads and pylons, linking people and spreading power and information; fragmenting habitats.

To understand these lines we need to recognise that they are of us, and that to ignore their social history is to remain blind to their significance today.

Beneficial, benign or malignant, these lines bind us and the natural world into an unnatural state. This state is not static: the good can be neglected, and the bad can be rewoven into the landscape. This is at the heart of this journey. How can we maximise the positive? We need to learn from the lines that have nurtured the landscape, and apply those lessons to help heal the scars. We need to learn to communicate without erecting barriers.

My train journey was coming to an end. The line of the border with Scotland had been unmarked. Hadrian's Wall was long gone too, but the linescapes were still around us. Even as we entered the wilder land, lanes and walls, hedges and ditches were all in evidence – a tangle of lines waiting to be read.

'One may liken the English landscape, especially in a wide view, to a symphony,' writes W. G. Hoskins near the beginning of his classic book *The Making of the English Landscape* – the more poetic and persuasive precursor to Pryor's – 'which it is possible to enjoy as an architectural mass of sound, beautiful or impressive as the case may be, without being able to analyse it in detail or to see the logical development of its structure.'

While I love to experience great symphonies washing over me, learning to read individual lines of music can open up new appreciation of the whole. And we will, I believe, see more deeply into the world around us if we learn to read the lines in our landscape. They are so much more than their function as barriers or carriageways. To change our perspective – towards an empathic look at the landscape – is to become aware of the impact they have, and the only way to really alter how we weave our lines.

1

Archaeological Lines

Reaves chequer Dartmoor. Relics of Bronze Age field systems, these low walls, often little more than hints of the linear features they once were, map out a story of lines that reaches forward from their origins 3,500 years ago to the present. When you can find them.

They are, though, by no means the earliest lines on our landscape. The 'Sweet Track',[1] unearthed in 1970, is the remains of a raised path between Westhay and Shapwick in Somerset built by Neolithic farmers in, we know with remarkable precision thanks to dendochronology, the study of tree rings to date timbers, either 3807 or 3806 BC. For a while it was thought to be the oldest track in the country, until in 2009 an even older one was found near Belmarsh Prison in south-east London. The Sweet Track was part of a network laid out to cross the boggy land and reach valuable 'islands' when the waters rose each winter. These paths required considerable communal effort to connect communities. The rich peat into which the wooden stakes were driven to carry the planks of the path reveals something of what the world was like 6,000 years ago. Hazelnuts, for example, have been found stored in a pot beside the track, and an indication of the status of the track is suggested by the discovery of a rare jadeite axe head. An axe of this sort was symbolic and valuable, made with stone from the Alps, and was probably placed as an offering.

These tracks tease us; they remind us how little we really know of what life was like before. And they remind us of how much evidence has been lost. The huts of ice-chasing Mesolithic hunter-gatherers, colonising the newly scoured, post-glacial land, have gone. They were replaced by Neolithic flints, Bronze Age villages, Iron Age hill forts, Roman roads, Anglo-Saxon cultivation, the Norman Conquest, and onwards to the modern era. The erosion of time, wind, water and life has leached the land of our ancestors' fingerprints.

Yet there are some places that seem to have managed to cling on to the past. And with that they carry a mystery that is enormously attractive. Rich in memories, thanks to a collision of geology and climate, Dartmoor is such a place. Though it looks wild, it has been a man-made landscape since the Neolithic. I find that hard to remember when I wallow in the magic of the place. My usually empirical mind will easily spot the spore of faerie in moss-rich crevices.

Ten thousand years ago the bleak sweep of moor was tree-clad. Early communities started the process of removing trees, initially to create clearings in which game would congregate to eat the succulent new-growth, and become far easier targets. As agriculture developed clearances became more focused, and by the Bronze Age the moor would have been productive farmland, demarcated by the reaves.

But then there was a change, and cultivation ceased. It seems likely a combination of reduced soil fertility and a wave of colder, wetter weather reduced the ability of the land to flourish, causing communities to move to lower ground.

The more benign land was not without field margins of stone. Reaves spread, during a flurry of building activity across the south of Britain that lasted just fifty or so years, marking the point in time in the Bronze Age when we began to use lines to assert ownership over the landscape and authority over nature.

But we have lost sight of most of them, thanks to the combination of integration – many modern field margins might be able to trace their history back to reaves, had we the skills to read the lines – and the scouring of agriculture, industry and housing.

Dartmoor's reaves survive because the land was never again cultivated with such intensity. Much of the stone has been sequestered for other work like houses and modern stone walls, but the essence of the reaves remains, even if it can sometimes be a challenge to find. I was looking forward so much to an excuse to wander in search of them.

I began my search after an evening with the Dartmoor photographer Simon Blackbourn. He showed me one of his beautiful photographs of the moor. 'You see there is a wall, but there is so much more to read into this – those lines, they are gorges left behind by tin mining after the seams were dug out; there, medieval terracing running perpendicular – and modern forestry. Not forgetting the buildings, roads, Neolithic monuments, a military training area and a bloody great TV transmitter. It always makes me smile when people call Dartmoor a "wilderness",' he said.

It was summer; the next morning the sky was richly blue and decorated by white horses tossing their manes, hinting at wind to come. And the vegetation on the moor was at its peak. Bracken had leapt from cute folk-club violin-head curls to overbearing Glastonbury crowds, obscuring all in its path. Including the reaves. A rudimentary mistake; turns out that they are only visible when the vegetation has died down.

I could not waste the opportunity, though; visits to the moor are all too rare. So I took time to explore some of the other memories held by the land, and set my course to a place called Grimspound. Simon had mentioned that this might be an interesting diversion, and it was near the spot where he had taken the image of a much-worked 'wilderness'.

I have never been able to just drive across Dartmoor. I am obliged to stop. There is always something to see, hear, scent. The meander I took to my destination wound me down to the River Dart, where I stopped. Walking along the tumbled boulders I was amazed at the water. Never has it looked more like whisky, glittering gold in July light. I could have stayed for hours. But I did have a mission, and managed to pull myself from this beautiful reverie.

I find it hard to understand why we are all so familiar with the charismatic megastars of the archaeological world, yet have managed to remain ignorant of the gems on Dartmoor. There was no fuss, no signpost, no map, no gift shop, no dedicated parking – just a regular narrow Dartmoor lane and fairly bare hills to either side. I pulled into a layby and started to walk uphill across tussocky grass. The heather held its pink-purple bells still as the wind whipped the grass stems into a blur. I came to a path: heavy stones laid into the ground. I was following the natural line, more steeply now, between the hills. Soon the path crossed a stone-clad ditch. This was a leat.

The lines of the leats are another engineering marvel that goes back to at least medieval times, when they were employed to guide water to power hammers that crushed tin ore. The water also powered the bellows used in smelting. There are hundreds of kilometres of leats across the moors, carrying water that was used by the farms for everything from drinking and washing to keeping food cool. Not the most sanitary of water distribution networks: the odd dead sheep could unsettle even the most iron constitution. Frequently they have been built with such subtlety, hugging contours, that they appear to be allowing water to flow uphill. In fact they were designed so carefully so as to reduce the risk of flooding when water was over-abundant.

So sidetracked was I by this beautifully engineered ditch that I had not lifted my head to see what was coming. At first there was just a line of broken-down wall, but as I carried on up the hill the line curved out into a smile and then the circle of stone that guards the remains of the late-Bronze-Age settlement of Grimspound. There was a small plaque that I assumed had some useful information about this unexpected delight. It told me to keep my horse out of the stone circle.

The wall, now a tumbled ruin, was once nearer 2 metres tall. And while the enclosure of 1.6 hectares is impressive, and the clearly defined main entrance is imposing, I was really struck by what was inside. The remains of twenty-four small huts are scattered throughout, and there were probably far more. One remained so well preserved (or possibly a little rebuilt – some of the early archaeologists were not as fastidious as those of today) that the porch was obvious, a J-shape that would have protected the interior from prevailing winds. I paced out a 3-metre diameter for these circular houses of stone.

The acid soil has done away with most of the organic memories, but the lichen-crusted stones present clues. Investigators, trowel-bearing time travellers, have scraped down and found some answers. Ash from the fireplaces, often in the centre of the homes, showed evidence of willow, oak and, predominantly, peat. This would indicate that the moor had lost much of its tree cover by the time Bronze Age families moved in. Peat takes a long time to accumulate, around 1 millimetre per year, so for there to be enough to provide fuel gives an indication of the changes in the landscape.

The wind whipping the clouds also pulled the temperature down to a point where it belied the beauty of the scene. But it was not 'grim', as the name suggested. The Saxon word *grimm* meant fierce or savage. But this was a relatively recent naming; no reference can be found before the late eighteenth century, and it must say more about the people's stories than the place itself. The two hills rising either side of Grimspound, one capped by Hookner Tor, give it a feeling of protection, if not from the elements, then from less corporeal threats. There is no mistaking the commanding presence of the tors, erupting from the land.

I walked up and away from Grimspound towards Hookner Tor and, after causing some ponies to lift their grass-nuzzling heads for a moment, with the air of locals in a very local pub being interrupted by the arrival of an outsider, I got to see a very different view. The path I had walked up to the tor carried straight on through the circle and up the other side, while the path which had led up from my car also passed clean through, and they met in the middle of Grimspound.

Tim Sandles, author of the fascinating website Legendary Dartmoor, points out that these are later paths – one specifically running to the nearby Vitifer tin mine and known as the 'Miners' Path' is thought to date from the thirteenth century. It is fascinating to be looking down on the footworn lines that have remained unchanged for the last 800 years at least. And off to my right, there were the thin gorges from tin mining and medieval terracing reminding me that this peopled land is newly empty.

But from this position, what struck so hard was that those circles were homes. Around 3,300 years ago, a little after the reaves I sought were built, people, possibly my ancestors, lived here. These people may have been 'reavers'.

There was a clattering noise behind me, and I turned to see a cloud of jackdaws raucously taking flight from the silhouetted tor.

*

In early December I had another opportunity to visit the moor and find the reaves, but the bracken, though dead, had not collapsed enough to be truly revealing. Simon suggested I explore an alternative Dartmoor site, Merrivale. At least these lines you cannot miss, he told me.

This time the weather was traditional drizzle, road-hugging cloud. I parked up in another layby and headed out into the grey. My heavy beard soon sucked so much moisture from the atmosphere that I could wring from it a small stream of water. I was beginning to reconsider my love affair with the moor. But it is important to see your paramour in every light. Another leat ran across my path, and as I climbed up the cloud lifted enough for me to see two stones set upright. As I got closer I could see that from them ran a double line of smaller stones. It looked like a case of bad dentistry: stubs sticking out at odd angles, but definitely in a line. About 25 metres to the south was another double line running in parallel. Up here on a hill, shrouded in water, was another mystery as impressive, imposing and impenetrable as the famous monuments of Wiltshire.

The lines were of different lengths, the northern one shorter at around 180 metres, the southern around 250 metres. And around them was so much more. There was a stone circle, there were 'cysts' (stone tombs with broken lids); there was a 3-metre-tall menhir. Halfway along the southern line there was a stone circle. Taking photographs and scribbling notes, I thrilled to be among some of the Bronze Age's most fascinating creations.

Though clearly important, explanations of Merrivale's

purpose remain largely guesswork. Writers from the nine-teenth century suggested it was a venue for chariot races or Druidical ceremonies, but neither existed until at least a thousand years after these stones had been erected. Possibly it formed some kind of ceremonial route, though most appealing is the idea of an astronomical calendar. What its stones are not, however, is reaves. They seem to have no practical function, and are certainly not part of any field boundaries.

The archaeologist Olaf Bayer came to my help. 'We describe the world in rational terms, aware of geology and geomorphology,' he explained to me, 'whereas our ancestors saw a landscape filled with agency, one that was animate. There were real reasons for doing things – appeasing gods was important, and it really is only in the post-war years that we have developed this habit of rationality. So it is a false dichotomy, the sacred and the profane. Theirs was prob-ably a pantheistic world, one in which there was spirit in everything.'

These worlds are met most famously at Stonehenge. This was built around 5,000 years ago in an environment already determined by paths and other lines. For example, the Cur-sus, running for 3 kilometres beside the more obvious monument, is a pair of lines that was probably a ceremonial pathway. And as our landscape reading skills have improved, so the links between henges and barrows have revealed a complex sacred landscape.

Stonehenge was built on other lines, older still and not of human origin at all: naturally occurring ridges shaped by the melt-water of retreating glaciers, which coincidentally point in one direction towards the mid-winter sunset, and in the other at the mid-summer sunrise.[2] We are blessed with this knowledge, but to an earlier people the significance must have been obvious.

It is worth remembering, given the human tendency to view the world in one way, and assume the current model is correct, that those who created these ancient monuments also knew that what they were doing was correct. And maybe future generations will look in wonder at how much we did not understand. Perhaps we should be a little less arrogant in assuming superiority.

*

The next time I was down on Dartmoor I hadn't even been thinking about trying to see the reaves. I was staying just outside Totnes in a happy jumble of a farmhouse with the ecologist Amy Grace-Fensome to watch the eagerly antici-pated solar eclipse the next day. But as I was thinking of where on the moor it would be good to see the eclipse and we started to look at maps and books, I remembered the reaves. In Oliver Rackham's *The History of the Countryside* I found Combestone Tor on the Holne to Hexworthy road, from which, if the vegetation was kind, apparently, reaves were visible. What better place to experience the eclipse than from on top of a tor!

The next day we headed off on our adventure under a duvet of cloud. As we drove up onto the moor I noticed a patch of brighter sky to my right. I glanced and then noticed that when I blinked, I could see a small memory of what I could not see – the sun with a nibble from its top right side.

And now it looked as though we might see the eclipse. In preparation we had made a device out of a box, gaffer tape and my binoculars. The merest glance had left its mark, so I was very happy to have a slightly virtual vision.

I caught a glimpse of the tor, just one valley beyond, looking more like petrified piles of laundry. Not deep into the moor, Combestone is famously accessible, and there was a silhouette of someone, legs wide, on top of its squat jumble of stones. In the car park we joined around a dozen other sightseers.

The Blue Peter-style gadget did not work. Maybe the sun was not bright enough, filtered through layers of cloud, to generate the expected beam, but at least the cloud did mean I could look briefly at the sun, possibly unwisely, and begin to see the change.

A skylark, my first of the year, was singing, and as I looked around me I saw, at last, the reaves. The lines of stone, or in some cases hints of lines of stone, were so low that I understood why previous adventures had been unsuccessful. But they were there – as they have been there since the Bronze Age, over 3,500 years ago.

From where I stood the most noticeable lines ran up the far side of the Dart valley, in remarkable parallel. Many hundreds of metres between these shadows of lines, and yet still they ran together. These were boundaries created with intent, not generated as a by-product of field-clearance: enclosures. As Olaf Bayer explained, the thinking nowadays is that these lines probably existed in the minds of the local people before they became physical. The enclosures – asserting ownership, we assume, were imagined all over the south of England until the notion of actually creating this linescape spread in such a short time.

Early commentators thought them relict trackways, possibly guiding Roman legionaries, but it was not until the beginning of the twentieth century that people began to formulate the idea of them being boundaries. The word reave comes from the old Saxon for line or row. And far from them being a trackway across the moor, there are over 400 kilometres that can be found over much of this magical landscape.[3]

As they dropped off the moor the reaves seemed to vanish, but this was just because Dartmoor is an island of preservation, a large lump of granite which has never been managed as it once was many thousands of years ago. And as with Grimspound and Merrivale, the wondering as to what life was like here so long ago threatened to exclude the eclipse. I had to force myself back to the celestial: the reaves would probably last out the next hour, but the eclipse would not be around again for quite a while.

It is hard to tell how much was chance and how much a result of the sliding moon. But the air felt colder as the sun shrank. And the skylark stopped singing, giving the gentle roar of the River Dart to our north greater presence in the aural mix. A coincidence? Around 90 per cent of the sun's light was blocked from reaching us – the dark side of the moon must have been rather less so. The time lag, about eight minutes for light to reach us from the sun, got me thinking astronomically. It takes about a million years for each of those photons to bounce their way from the centre of that fusion reactor in the sky to its edge, and release and freedom. So by the time we catch them they are already very old. Some, indeed, travel much further. One cold, clear night the previous winter, I found myself stopped at a puddle in the towpath of the Thames in Oxford, staring at Jupiter in the water. Jupiter does not shine; it reflects. A photon of light that has left the surface of the sun after a million-year-flight from the core leaps into space and travels for 43 minutes before hitting the surface of Jupiter and then bouncing back towards the earth for another 35 minutes, whereupon it uses the surface of the puddle for one last journey into my eye, onto my retina and then onwards as an electrical impulse to my slightly overwhelmed brain.

Despite the clouds shifting slowly there were glimpses of the sun in its reduced state. We borrowed a fellow gawper's special eclipse viewer – she had spent ages searching Totnes and beyond before finding it, all for her four-year-old son who had expressed such excitement and was now ignoring the proceedings with equal concentration. The vision was extraordinary, with our star appearing like a waxing moon, or a slightly lopsided smile.

Without the distraction of artificial light the sky becomes all. The early gods were sky gods, and why not? At night, when fear has real cause, the movement of the stars and planets must provide escape for the mind. So the Bronze Age builders whose reaves, lines and circles remain as testament to their labour must have watched these celestial moments struck with awe.

Gradually the light breeze seemed to soften, or rather warm, and then the skylark was up, welcoming back the fuller light of the day, or the warmer air, or just re-asserting ownership of that patch of land. As I turned to clamber down the tor back towards the car I noticed, just across the narrow lane, two more reaves. From ground level I probably would not have seen them, but now they were obvious. I went and walked along them, and was struck by how gold the short, pony-cropped grass looked – maybe more copper actually, with a smattering of verdigris: hints of spring coaxing a patina of new life from the moor.

In photographs of these reaves, though visible they remain a little like a shape in low light, best viewed out of the corner of your eye. It is as if too much concentration on these relicts makes them shy away from attention, so used are they to being ignored.

Well, not totally ignored. One reason they are so insubstantial is the value later inhabitants of the moor saw in their neatly stacked stones, and many have since been appropriated into newer walls and homes. Though not so much as to completely eradicate all trace. We can see the reaves on Dartmoor thanks to the collision of factors that has preserved them in a state of limbo; not quite gone, not quite there. But it is the image of them tumbling off the moor into life and our modern lives that I love.

These cryptic monuments to the Bronze Age were not the first to be built into the land. And they are vastly diminished.

But even in this residual state they carry with them the hint of what was to come. The origin of so much that disturbs and disrupts our ecosystems had its inception in these long lines of rock. The idea that sprang them into life was the same idea that created hedges, walls, fences and all the barriers that accommodate or restrict wildlife. As Mesolithic people, hunting and gathering, began to settle into the Neolithic and the Bronze Age, so did the need to demarcate land they owned – as well as restrain livestock, keeping crop and stock separate. The compartmentalisation of our country had begun.

2

Hedges

Of all the habitats I have encountered it is with the hedge that I feel most at home. It was in a hedge that I hid as a kid, and where I found myself being observed by a fox. It was hidden by hedges that I found out about sex. And it was along hedges that I followed one of the constants in my life.

It seems like a perfect match, hedgehogs and hedges – after all, there is little mystery in the name of the animal I have studied for so long. It is an animal that loves to hog the hedges. The real origin of the word 'hedge', however, is more interesting and delightfully circular. *Haag* is Dutch for enclosure. *Hagen* is Middle High German for thorn. *Haga* is Old English for haw. Hawthorn is the oldest of the hedgerow trees – and the hedgehog the main animal of the hedge. The hedgehog being covered in thorn; living within thorn.

Delving into the etymological maze got me wondering whether 'hag' had been derived from the same root – and whether this was another instance of misappropriation. Hawthorn, the writer Jay Griffiths pointed out to me, was a deeply important tree of northern European pagan religion, and the Hægtesse was a powerful mythical woman once associated with divination, healing and cursing, whose name stems from what we now call a hedge. 'It could be that the Hægtesse were hedge-riders,' she told me, 'which could either be a literal reading of the fact that women with perceived power would live beyond the bounds of the civilised world of the village as defined by the border provided by a hedge. Or it could be a more esoteric vision: that these were women with a foot on either side of the hedge that separates the physical from the spiritual domains.'

Though designed to keep things apart, I always consider the hedge as a place of meeting. The hedge is an edge, and in habitat terms specifically an analogue for woodland edge: the rich, liminal zone between the meadow and the woodland. Lines like these have the greatest diversity. Life that needs the edges of woodland craves both the light and the shade. There are flowers, insects and birds that find this interworld a sanctuary.

The dunnock, misnamed as a hedge sparrow, scuttles like a mouse from the base of the sheltering hedge. Ramsons rumble out of woodland along the hedgerows, breaking new ground. Skippers, whites, hairstreaks, ringlets and gatekeepers dance in this lengthy woodland edge. At night, feeding along this linear buffet, pipistrelles, Daubenton's and Natterer's bats skitter beside serotines, brown long-eareds and horseshoes.

Hedges all share the same origins – barriers that assert ownership, restrain livestock and separate from the wild – and have a great history. 'The most ancient authors preferred a living hedge to a constructed fence,' wrote the first-century-BC agricultural writer Columella, 'because it not only called for less expense, but was more permanent and lasted for an indefinite time.' Julius Caesar, in around 55 BC, gives one of the first references to the practice of laying a hedge, writing in *The Gallic Wars* of the Nervii tribe in Flanders, who would create a barrier to obstruct an assault by cavalry. 'They cut into slender trees and bent them over so that many branches came out along their length; they finished these off by inserting brambles and briars, so that these hedges formed a defence like a wall, which could not only not be penetrated but not even be seen through.'

The first reference to the hedges that now give Britain its distinctive check pattern comes from AD 547, to one erected by Ida of Northumbria around his new settlement of Bamburgh,[1] but the presence of the Dartmoor reaves, and the knowledge of how far they really spread, would suggest they have been around for far longer.

Hedges begin to be recorded more systematically in the eleventh-century *Domesday Book*, though often these are within references to 'woodland for hedges', suggesting that there was a need to accumulate vegetation for dead-hedging – as opposed to living hedges that are to some extent self-perpetuating. Even a dead hedge, though, a barrier of thorn held together by stakes, has the potential to generate life by providing a shelter for seedlings to take root.

Those early documents also reveal the obligations placed by the manors on common folk – requiring them to provide time, as well as poles or stakes, to keep hedges in order. And also to make sure that the hedges do not cause too much habitat fragmentation . . . for an elite few. In the twelfth century Richard I issued a decree that boundary structures should not be so high as to interfere with the hunt.

Oliver Rackham teases out the details of hedge history in Britain, finding charters back in the eighth century referring to them, and one in 816 referring to what was already an 'old hedge'.[2] Clearly more than just livestock restraint devices, they also form boundaries; ways in which land can be apportioned. And as we will see from the green lanes in chapter 5, they are an integral component of the early transport infrastructure: a defining feature of a green lane is that it is bounded on at least one side by a hedge.

Sometimes, though, a hedge has a different purpose. The 'Penny Hedge' tradition in Whitby derives from a legend dating back to 1159. Three noblemen out hunting a boar followed it to a hermitage, where the resident monk gave the fleeing animal sanctuary. Frustrated, the hunters killed the monk, and the lands and lives of these blood-crazed fools were spared only thanks to the dying wishes of the monk and the generous spirit of the abbot. However, they had to commit to a penance: every Rogation Wednesday, the eve of Ascension Day, they had to build a short hedge, strong enough to withstand three tides, cutting hazel stakes with a knife bought for a penny. I am not sure if the final stipulation still holds, but every year the hedge is still built.

Like all the lines in this book, hedges are dynamic – they have always changed, in purpose and in style. For a time, in the crushing industrialisation of agriculture that succeeded the end of the last war, it seemed they might slip into memory altogether, along with their ancestors. But the onslaught was reined in and not everything was lost, though still there are hedge-wraiths, barely present hedges reminding us how close we have come to their demise.

There is more at stake than just the loss of their physical entity. The process of managing a hedge so it thrives in its local environment has evolved over many generations. A break in the story can fragment the passage of knowledge, something known as the 'extinction of experience.'[3] All over the world agricultural systems are being disrupted by this erosion – the loss of language, or just words, to describe, own and manage the land.

One of the great 'extinctions of experience' came with the dramatic shedding of people from the land through the process of the enclosures. Through acts of law enclosures transformed public and common land into private land. While they had been used since the thirteenth century, they reached their peak between 1750 and 1830, when around 4,000 acts of parliament were passed, handing land from the community to the wealthy. The granting of the enclosure came with a requirement for a boundary to be maintained. This had the consequence of ensuring larger landowners benefited, as the proportion of length to area decreases with the size of holding, thus reducing costs of hedge, fence or wall maintenance. The agents of enclosure were most often hedges. Put up as they now were on a more industrial scale, they became more monotonous: straighter, more rectangular, not the organic meandering of earlier years.

The evidence of these enclosures can still be seen today. Regular fields with straight hedges tend to come from that time. There is no doubting that hedge-loving wildlife will at the time have benefited greatly from these new corridors. It was at this time too that the numbers of hedgerow trees were at their greatest – a valuable source of timber for those allowed to harvest them. A 'pension tree' was a tree that a worker was allowed to leave to grow in the length of hedge that was his responsibility, and then harvest when he retired or became too ill to work. Such trees provided a source of fuel or income.

Hedgerow trees continue to make a vital contribution to the biodiversity of such lines: over half the species of conservation concern found within the hedge are dependent on the emergent trees. Woodpeckers need mature wood for food and shelter. Bats use hedges to navigate along and the tree to roost in. Hedges with trees have 60 per cent more larger moths than those without. Epiphytes such as lichen and moss need trees, and fungal variety will always be richer where there is wood to rot.

Hedges link wildlife and nurture people, but they have also fragmented society. The consequences of the enclosures were dramatic. It is argued by some that they were the necessary kindling for the Industrial Revolution. Crop yields and productivity increased, releasing labour for industry. Conversely, the enclosures are also seen as an act of 'class robbery'.[4]

Criticism of the enclosures began long before they became so commonplace. In 1516, Sir Thomas More argues in *Utopia* that the act of taking land from the community normalised theft.

the nobility and gentry, and even those holy men, the abbots not contented with the old rents which their farms yielded, nor thinking it enough that they, living at their ease, do no good to the public, resolve to do it hurt instead of good. They stop the course of agriculture, destroying houses and towns – reserving only the churches – and enclose grounds that they may lodge their sheep in them.

But the most heartfelt plea came from the hedgerow poet, John Clare, whose own world was enclosed. His words conjure a post-apocalyptic scene.

And hedgerow briars – flower lovers overjoyed
Came and got flower pots – these all destroyed
And sky bound mores in mangled garb are left
Like mighty giants of their limbs bereft.
Fence now meets fence in owners' little bounds
Of fields and meadow large as garden grounds
In little parcels little minds to please
With men and flocks imprisoned ill at ease.[5]

In 1966, the writer Arthur Raistrick described the enclosures as 'a tragedy for the common people; they lost their rights on the communal meadow, lost their plots of land and were forced to become waged workers at a time of falling wages and rising costs of living. Enclosures made sure that the working classes became slaves.'

The actively enclosed fields conferred a very different character on the land, one we now have come to accept as our traditional landscape. But it was not that long ago when people would read the lines across it and see the history more clearly. 'It is but five grassy acres,' writes Edward Thomas in his essay, 'One Green Field', published in 1906,

> and yet as the stile admitting you to it makes you pause – to taste the blackberries or to see how far the bryony has twined – you salute it in a little while as a thing of character. Many of the fields around are bounded by straight-ruled hedges, as if they had been cut up by a tyrant or a slave, with only a few of such irregularities as a stream or a pond may enforce. Not one of the five hedges of this field makes a straight line. The hedge up to your right from the stile is of a noble and fascinating unruliness.[6]

For all the wildness they might suggest, hedges are, above all, man-made, and monuments of history. But in making them we increase the biodiversity of the surrounding land. Leave a hedge alone and it will do its best to erupt into a line of trees, and in that act of exuberance kill the idea of the hedge. Hedges are like domestic animals; they need assistance to survive. Even when that assistance looks rather brutal – perhaps this could be seen as a metaphor for the enclosures as well – it can also be beneficial.

The most refined art of management comes in the form of hedge laying. When I lived in Manchester I used to join a group of conservation volunteers and we would head out armed with billhooks, axes, bow saws and a modicum of training. The work was hard, frequently accompanied by hangover-shredding Sunday weather. But the delight in seeing a stretch of grown-out hedge, lying down, temporarily obedient and domesticated, was intense.

This involves nearly severing the trunks of near-trees and laying them down along the hedge line. It is important to keep just enough living wood to allow the tree to keep growing, sprouting new growth, vertically, to create what we recognise as a hedge. Leaving too much risks the trunk splitting. The woven structure of resting trees provides one of the richest wildlife habitats in the country.

And then would come the fire; the piling of brashings, the offcuts of the thorn trees, along with some of the more bulky wood, into a blaze that undid the chill. Cups of tea and occasionally foil-covered potatoes baked in its heart – a perfect end to a weekend. Now, I gather, there is a tendency to use this wood for habitats, which is great for wildlife, less so for the volunteers.

I knew at the time I was laying crudely. I had seen photographs of how it should look and, really, my stretches were never going to win any prizes. And yes, there are prizes to be won. In 2015, I was very lucky to be invited to run a stall at the National Hedge Laying Championships.

Here, along the edges of a field in Lincolnshire, I found over a hundred men and three women (this is as yet a largely unreconstructed hobby), each with 10 metres of trees to transform into a hedge in just five hours. This competition was the highest expression of a subculture that could easily fade away. And losing this experience would require all hedging to be done from the back of a tractor.

Feeling somewhat mournful at the potential loss of such a special skill and all that it brings to wildlife, I headed out into the buzz of competition to remind myself that people really do care, and found an accelerated version of what was once a mainstay of rural life. The busyness and accuracy of the competitors put my feeble attempts truly in their place. Depending on the style of hedge, one or both sides got trimmed into a vertical face with a chainsaw before the work of part-felling began – setting in place a structure that can grow into a multidimensional wall of life.

It seems there is a good reason why this unlikely act of regeneration takes place. These trees have adapted over millions of years to tolerate the presence of large herbivores. Elephants, for example, knock over trees to get at the foliage. Now, if every tree that was elephanted died, we would soon have a desert. But if, when part-felled, the trees continue to live and indeed sprout new life, herbivores can be fed again, and disaster is averted. So the question has to be asked: why are so many trees in Britain so good at coping with this sort of attention? For without that capabiliity we would not have a hedge-veined landscape – we would not have coppiced or pollarded woodlands, woodlands which supplied the charcoal that, it could be argued, kickstarted the Industrial Revolution. Yet where are the elephants?

In his fascinating, revolutionary book *Feral*, George Monbiot points out that the very fact our trees have evolved to cope with such a beating is evidence, supported by clear fossil records, that this land was once populated by an amazing array of herbivorous megafauna.

Most of the deciduous trees in Europe can re-sprout wherever the trunk is broken. They can survive the extreme punishment – hacking, splitting, trampling – inflicted when a hedge is laid. Understorey trees such as holly, box and yew have much tougher roots and branches than canopy trees, despite carrying less weight. Our trees, in other words, bear strong signs of adaptation to elephants. Blackthorn, which possesses very long spines, seems over-engineered to deter browsing by deer; but not, perhaps, rhinoceros.[7]

The art of hedge laying is highly regional. Everywhere has its own style, dictated by the climate, geology and habit. There are over thirty styles recognised around Britain alone, and more further afield, that have evolved to meet the needs of the land and the farming practice. The Midland Bullock, for example, is designed to withstand the weight of cattle and horses that might push against the hedge. Thick stems are part-split and leant over. Branches on the side of the hedge facing the crop are removed, while on the other side the brush is left to provide extra protection against livestock. Stakes are driven into the ground at regular intervals, and hazel binders weave the line together for extra support.

The Welsh Border hedge is distinguished by the stakes being driven in at a 35-degree angle 30 inches apart, and the use of dead wood to protect both sides from browsing by stock. The Derbyshire hedge is more like a Midland Bullock, but lower and without bindings, whereas the Devon is normally laid on top of a bank. This world can get a little involved.

Back at my stall, I finished sorting out the leaflets from the British Hedgehog Preservation Society and propped the 'Please touch, but be sensible, it will hurt if you do it the wrong way,' notice beside my stuffed hedgehog. Next to me was a man from the Country Landowners' Association. I was apprehensive that this might result in a rather lengthy argument.

Perhaps surprisingly there was common ground. Hedgehog conversation swiftly, and predictably, moved onto badgers – surely I was in favour of a cull, he suggested, if only to help hedgehogs? Normally at nine in the morning, and with a slight hangover, I would smile and walk away, but we were destined to be together for hours, so I thought I would have a go at explaining the complex ecological state that exists between these two species.

The badger is a natural predator of the hedgehog. But predation is not the only relationship they have. Hedgehogs and badgers compete for the same food: they are both macro-invertebrate specialists – they eat worms and other small animals as a preference. So they are competitors. However, once this food source is compromised their relationship shifts to predation.

The relationship with badgers is further complicated by the ability of brock to fragment the landscape. Radio-tracking work has shown that hedgehogs dispersing radially along hedgerows from a village will stop and retreat when they come across badger activity. The fewer and thinner the hedges, the greater the chance hedgehogs will find a latrine or a sett. Which is why I am such a fan of hedge laying – the more hedges that get managed properly, the more habitat there is for hedgehogs. The hogging of the hedge is real – research has shown how hedgehogs in the Netherlands spent 87% of their lives within just 5 metres of a hedge.

There is an additional problem: farmers have been inadvertently farming badgers, with great success. Subsidies paid for maize production have encouraged its planting, and over the last twenty-five years the area under cultivation has increased to around 160,000 hectares. This can reduce the macro-invertebrates in the soil through the use of agrochemicals and soil compaction, making life tough for both species, but the badgers have an advantage: they love maize. That, combined with a long run of mild winters, which leads to a greater survival rate for youngsters in January and February, has allowed the population to flourish. They enter winter with greater fat reserves, and therefore more survive. It does not take long before this results in the sort of population increases we have seen in Britain. And while there are some badger lovers who resist the reality and want to downplay badger numbers to help support their opposition to various inarticulate culls, the number of setts has certainly increased by around 100% in the last twenty-five years.

So how did I end up in agreement with the CLA? If the land is managed well there will be macro-invertebrates enough to go around, but instead the land is hammered because some farmers get paid such a small amount for what they produce and, in turn, squeeze what they can from their land at a terrible ecological cost. So, I argued, it was the supermarkets who were at the heart of the problem – and there, we both decided, in accord, we should cease from politics, just in case, and retired to our stalls.

Sat then with a cup of tea, mulling over the question of hedges, I was struck by how, as so often with management of our wilder places, you have to almost break things to make them better. Coppicing and pollarding, when certain trees are cut at ground level or head height respectively, and then sprout forth in grand profusion, are more examples. Yet to the untrained eye, the management can seem quite barbaric until the wonderful transformation erupts.

Walking into another marquee I noticed a man sat in the corner behind a table full of books with the air of someone holding court, surrounded by a considerable bustle. I moved into the crowd and found myself in the presence of the German academic and author Georg Muller. As I talked to him through his interpreter and friend Jef Gielen, I found a man of remarkable dedication. Over a period of 35 years Georg has visited 32 countries, driven 240,000 kilometres, walked 20,000 more, and taken over 50,000 photographs, all to research and measure the field boundaries of Europe. The resulting two-volume work he published, *Europe's Field Boundaries*, has 1,280 pages, 4,433 photos and 1,381 other illustrations. The scope of this amazing work is far greater than even the enormous distances travelled would suggest. Georg has recorded 170 different kinds of earth bank, 160 stone-faced banks, 10 peat banks, 330 field walls, 240 hedge styles, 70 dead brushwood hedges – and that is not counting the stick picket, vertical branch and wattle fences. So much of my reading on the hedgerow has been restricted to Britain, so the opening-out of the subject is one of the delights of Muller's work.

'I am aware of the fact that I am describing a dying cultural landscape,' he told me. 'I started out mapping and taking photographs in my homeland of Ganderkesse in the north-west of Lower Saxony. I had returned in 1977 to look for rare mushrooms. They are my first love. And I found that many of the hedge banks in which I had found them before were gone. I started mapping them a little later, and then when an academic was criticised for describing the destruction of this landscape, I made it my task to provide incontrovertible evidence.'

His work, which involved detailed examination of historical documents and maps as well as the measuring of current hedges, revealed what was evident to all those who cared to look. Eighty per cent of hedges present in 1842 were gone, and of the remainder only 0.8 per cent were in good condition.

There is inspiration in Muller's work as profound as that in John Clare's. Georg reaches into our conscience as well. He quotes 'the Poet of the Heath', Hermann Lons, the German writer and naturalist, and another casualty of the slaughter of the First World War, who in 1912 wrote:

It is not only the face of the landscape that loses its most beautiful features through the grubbing of hedged banks. It is not only the animal kingdom that suffers from it. The farmer's inside world will also hardly take a turn to better, if the essential character of his land goes down the drain. His inner nature will go barren, barren and poor, as all those folks will turn, whose land has not got more to offer than bread and money. Then, when it is too late, people will realise what they did when they put an end to the hedged banks.[8]

It is plain to see that the hedges of our countryside are in a poor condition. But at 500,000 kilometres in length, there are more now than before the beginning of the enclosures, when Oliver Rackham estimated there were just 320,000 kilometres. Peak hedge came in the mid-nineteenth century, as the enclosures came to an end, with around 800,000 kilometres of hedgerow. The extent of the nation's hedges stayed fairly constant until the rush to industrialise the countryside that came with the end of the Second World War. Since then at least 300,000 have gone.

Rapacious grubbing-up to earn payments from Europe has been replaced with nudges to nurture, but massive damage has still been done to this fecund network. And neglect continues its war of attrition, with the total length of actively managed hedge falling by 26,000 kilometres in the decade to 2007.

I am not out doing fieldwork these days, though there was a time as I tracked the trail of hedgehogs that I felt the hedge my second home. Now I spend my hedge time in the company of family and friends. And, like the hedgehogs, we are edge-specialists, keeping to the borders, not traipsing into crops.

The difference between these hedges and the domesticated versions that bound our gardens is as great as between a poodle and a wolf: related, but distantly so. One tame, the other fairly wild. But we can wild up our hedges at home if we put our mind to it: they can become rich habitats and natural corridors. If you are thinking about creating some new lines at home, consider planting more than beech and privet. Hedges can provide shelter for wildlife – and food for both you and wildlife. So get excited and get planting. And avoid what Oliver Rackham described so eloquently as 'the Vandal hand of tidiness'.

In my garden the hedge is dying. It came with the house, and has been retreating down the garden a few plants a year. The privet has provided food for insects and shelter for sparrows, who chatter like a class of children until you walk too close, and then, as if the teacher has come into the room, silence descends. The privet is also where the robins practise. At least, that is what it is assumed they do, singing so quietly that the sound seems to be coming from some distance – until you spot the orange breast and the beak imperceptibly moving. It is called sub-song. When we get to planting a new line, a fence will be necessary while it grows to keep our dream dog in.

And this is how it is in the countryside too. Frequently the hedge will now be augmented with a fence. I was driving through the fertile borders of Dartmoor when I came across a recently cropped hedge. In fact, the flail was at work only a short way ahead of me. The hedge reminded me of US marines – buzz-cut and angular. But beneath the muscular exterior was a hint of inner weakness – a wooden fence, showing signs of decay, and beyond it, a wire fence too.

I was stooped taking photographs when I realised the tractor had stopped and a robust figure was walking towards me. His posture spoke of defensiveness, but he relaxed as he learned of my interest in the lines in the land. He talked about his cutting regime, how he would cut frequently to maintain the hedge's thickness. He was dismissive of those with poorly maintained equipment – blunt blades lead to more tearing of the limbs rather than slicing. He liked his hedges neat, and used them as a calling card, as he supplemented his farm-income with contract hedge maintenance.

That style of management cannot last for ever: there will need to be additional planting and even laying to keep the hedge from redundancy. As the fencing suggests, this is something that might have happened already. Without management we will lose our hedges and, despite them not being unique to Britain, I do feel rather proprietorial about them. They are 'our' landscape feature. They capture the essence of Britain; they are the constraint of wildness, and they are in need of a bit of love and attention.

It is not unreasonable to consider the death sentence of the hedge as having been signed in the USA in 1874, when the businessman Joseph Glidden invented barbed wire. Portable and efficient, the wire reached Europe in 1885, at a time when much of the countryside's labour force had moved to the cities to feed the Industrial Revolution.

Barbed wire transformed the ranching life of the American prairies. Prior requirements of fencing had for many made it prohibitively expensive to establish new farms. But there was a downside: the wire was so easy to use that it fragmented the cattle routes and reduced access to water. Most alarming was the 'big die-up' of the winter of 1885. A long stretch of barbed wire had been strung up in Texas from east to west. Cattle began to move south as some of the worst winter weather on record hit – only to encounter this new fencing. When the blizzard eased thousands of animals were found dead up against the wire. As these enclosures changed farming for ever they also spelled the end of the subculture of the cowboy.[9]

Perhaps surprisingly, while wire fences tend to replace hedges, they can also encourage them too. In the United States, where the trend was to build fences out of barbed wire, they now have more miles of hedgerow than we do in Britain. Fence lines since the 1880s have acted as shelter for the seeds of trees and shrubs, which have sprung up and taken over the responsibility of sectioning the land.[10] The phenomenon is not restricted to the USA, but it seems to require an absence of management to take hold, which in crowded Britain is something of a rarity.

Another way in which hedgerows can appear without the need to plant them is when woodland is cleared to create a field, but with a line of trees left at the margin. Such fields would originally have been 'assarts' – clearances of forest (or heath) granted by the crown to landowners – and their relic hedges will still be identifiable to those who know what to look for: an assemblage of plants that hark back to the days when the hedge was just the edge of a woodland. Bluebell, primrose, wood anemone, dog's mercury and yellow arch-angel all attest to this former life.

I think hedges are one of the wonders of our semi-natural world. They can contain a fantastic abundance and diversity of life. If you doubt me, shift your perspective into the midst of the hedge itself and try and develop an empathy for not just other animals, but an entire ecosystem. Like taking a hand lens to a flower or small insect, there is a sudden revelation. There is so much more to life than that which is easily seen.

But we need to remember that hedges are an artifice – made and maintained by people. And there is a cost to having a hedge. Finding the value of a hedge is a complex matter. Economists would draw up a cost–benefit analysis and probably find the hedge wanting, which is why it is useful to have ecologists involved as well. For the farmer, a hedge has to be factored into a complex equation that will include both, to be sure, but also a general predisposition born of a myriad prejudices, just like those that inform my attitude to hedges.

The farming community likes to be recognised as a protector of the countryside, and frequently points out that without its efforts we would not have the beautiful mosaic of life we can still see. It is understandable, perhaps, for a farmer to become complacent. Their garden might have birds skittering around the feeder, bats skirting the night air on waves of silent sound – the myth of the countryside confirmed by the view from the kitchen sink. But that garden will often be an oasis amidst a desert of industry, a refuge linked by the linescapes still managed. Most wildlife on a farm – plant, animal and fungi – is found only at its margins, in the hedges, walls and ditches.

Farmers need to earn the role of protector if they truly want to be recognised as more than mere factory janitors.

Why would a farmer choose a hedge? At the Hedge Laying Championships I decided to go for another walk. These were increasingly tense fields. Some of the more experienced layers were already working on the finer detail, checking the binding along the top, and, for the third time, that the line of supporting stakes was straight. Others looked rather forlornly at trees still-standing. One man was lagging behind – I had stopped earlier to chat and admire his array of nicely sharpened and polished tools, and ruffle his spaniel's fur. Now his wife was standing guard. 'He's done nowt but natter,' she said, making quite sure I did not interrupt any more. Periodic, and increasingly desperate, bursts of chainsaw cut through the not very calm air.

Out in the real world, obviously, hedges are managed in a less frantic manner, but still, this is very hard work. Working my way around the fields I was able to pick up a few facts that put things into perspective.

Maintaining a hedge is not cheap, and unless you are lucky enough to arrange for a competition to be held on your land, hedge-laying costs around £12.50 per metre, and a skilled layer could manage 20 metres in a day. If you decide that's too much, then tractor-based hedge cutting costs around £320 per day and can cover 3 miles. And this is if there is already a hedge in place. If not, planting one provides no instant result, so if there was to be any livestock in the field you would have to supplement it with fencing. And if you are fencing already, why bother with the hedge?

Farmers will always grumble, but there are some really good reasons to grumble about hedges. Fences are so much more flexible. If you have a hedge, well, that is where the hedge is, unless you are going to destroy it to allow for the economy of scale offered by a larger field. And all that land that is under hedge is not under crop: around 500,000 kilometres of hedgerow in Britain, with an average width of 2 metres – that makes 100,000 hectares on which you can't grow anything. There is also the 'headland effect' – the impact of a hedge on the crop adjacent to it – which can result in up to a 19 per cent reduction in yield compared to the middle of a field. Though this might not all be down the hedge, and could be due to the compaction of soil where the machinery turns, there is a real competition between hedge and crop for water, light and nutrients.

And this is before we get onto hedges' role as reservoirs of insect pests – some of which feed on hedgerow plants in the spring before heading out into the fields for the summer. Oh, and to top it all, the leeward side of a hedge is sheltered. A good thing, you might think. But no, some insects end up being dumped into this sheltered patch, including nasties like aphids. In fact, there have been active campaigns against hedges. In the early nineteenth century the Royal Agricultural Society published a number of polemics, including 'On the necessity for the reduction or abolition of hedges'.

Fortunately, there are plenty of reasons to love the hedge. According to Nick Sotherton, Director of Research at the Game and Wildlife Conservation Trust, for example, 'Famous fox-hunting counties like Leicestershire are characterised by the small fields and hedged boundaries to provide opportunities for fox hunting.' It is a sad reality that one of the principal motivations for maintaining hedges is to maintain cover for blood sports. In fact, in some parts of the country the tops of hedges are specifically woven in such a way as to facilitate 'sport'. Research that Sotherton cites indicates that farms and estates which engaged in hunting and shooting planted and managed more hedges compared to those that did not, despite equal subsidies. But if the odd and cruel behaviour of a few can produce massive benefits to the wider countryside, can it be justified?

Luckily, there is plenty more in favour of the hedge. To go straight to what counts, farms with hedges sell for a higher price than those that are open prairie. Then there are the obvious things: hedgerows provide shelter for livestock – at some distance, too. Research showed that the shelter can extend out up to 16 times the height of the hedge. Livestock on farms without shelter have higher mortality and require more food. That shelter means the ground is warmer, so the growing season for grass is longer.

Caring about hedges is not just an ecological affectation of modern times. Georg Muller quotes this from Germany in 1829: 'In the course of the grubbing-up of hedgerows and coppices, various species of birds, which feed on the berries, would become extinct, and such an extinction would have no useful value, as they devour pests that are a threat to the farmer and, on balance, amounts to more than the bird takes away.'[11]

The list of benefits continues. Hedges reduce soil

erosion – they help soil retain moisture when there are drying winds that might otherwise whisk the topsoil away. And they keep the soil within the field. And while some pests may be harboured by a hedgerow there are also beneficial animals in it too. A rich flora in your hedge base will attract a host of predatory and parasitic species able to tackle crop pests – and not just the ones enticed by the hedge.

Clearly all this will be threatened if agrochemicals are sprayed directly at the hedge, or drift from careless application. Deliberate spraying of broad-spectrum herbicides at hedge bottoms was banned in 2005, but that does not leave them immune. Research from Oxford University has shown the great benefit to farmers when they keep their sprays well away from hedges and their margins. Not only is it a waste of costly chemicals, but fertilisers will also increase the nutrient level of the soil, resulting in an ecologically impoverished flora dominated by weeds, which will damage the crop.[12]

The strip of land along many field boundaries can play a vital role in maintaining and increasing farmland biodiversity. Such strips are one of the easier ways for farmers to receive extra payments from the stewardship schemes that manage grants from Europe. And while the very broad and shallow 'entry-level' schemes are often unrewarding to wildlife, in many cases the more targeted 'higher-level' schemes exceed expectation, creating far more ecological value.

There has been plenty of debate as to whether biodiversity benefits are best achieved by leaving fields alone – 'set aside' – or by using the boundaries and margin. The former has an advantage in that the areas of land in question are often larger; the latter, however, has the potential not only for wildlife gain in itself, but also to deliver wider landscape connectivity. Such gains are very cost-effective.

Nature conservation has, I believe, the greatest value of all, yet it is not the one most readily inscribed into the accounting ledgers. How do we ascribe financial value to the dusky thorn, the lackey and the garden tiger – moths that have experienced declines of over 90 per cent in the last forty years? The culprit has been agricultural intensification – something so much easier to insert into a balance sheet. If hedges and their margins are managed with care for a higher value, such species can be saved.

Just as I am prejudiced in favour of hedges, so am I also against relying upon the mechanisms that are tearing the fabric of life on the planet to pieces being used to patch it up again. Trusting capitalism to conserve nature is a bit like turning in the midst of a battle to the arms manufacturers for first aid.

Some of the greatest thinkers in the environmental world disagree, and certainly the issue of 'natural capital' is not easy to dismiss in its entirety. I can see that taxing carbon at source, for example, must be a good thing. But as for the argument that we can effectively legitimise destructive developments through 'off-setting' (the creation of what is deemed to be compensatory habitat elsewhere), well, it still strikes me as nothing more than glorified greenwash, to cover up the ecological sins of those who will carry on regardless. The radical eco-farmer Rebecca Hosking puts it more succinctly: 'It is all rather grubby.'

Two of the most eloquent combatants in this debate are the environmental campaigner and writer Tony Juniper and the *Guardian* columnist George Monbiot. He draws an analogy with how the mainstream political parties have become indistinguishable variations on the theme of rapacious neo-liberal capitalism. The mistake he sees is in thinking that to appeal to the other side you must make yourself more like them:

> because our opponents don't share our values and they are the people wrecking the environment, we have to go over to them and insist that we're really in their camp. All we care about is money. We don't really care about nature for its own sake. We don't really believe in any of this intrinsic stuff. We don't believe in wonder and delight and enchantment. We just want to show that it's going to make money.[13]

An exhilarating intellectual exchange on the subject took place between Juniper and Monbiot at the New Networks for Nature – itself the epicentre of ecocentric thinking. And while the argument in favour of a capitalised wild was well made – every other strategy has failed to halt the relentless decline of nature – George was able to present a far more nuanced vision; one that required us to consider the impact of 'framing' – how thinking about a subject from one particular perspective skews our ability to view it from another. The insidious effect of 'framing' nature as a resource with a financial value is that it requires nature to be considered as a resource to be traded and, as such, 'owned'. It no longer has an intrinsic value – something hard to define, like love – and instead only an extrinsic, commercial value that can be calculated.

*

We miss most things because we are too big and too fast. We can't shrink, but we can slow down. Spending a little more time in the company of nature to begin to see quite how much we are missing is a wonderful thing. Down in Devon, therefore, Robert Walton, the chairman of the Devon Hedge Group, has undertaken a study of a single hedge on his farm, with the simple aim of trying to count the number of different species in it. Simple, in conception; in practice, massively difficult. He set some straightforward parameters. The species had to be big enough to see with the naked eye, and be on or within 2 metres of the tips of shrubs and trees in the hedge. He spent two years on it.

Only 85 metres long and 6.5 metres wide between the widest margins, this hedge has at its heart, like most Devon hedges, an earth bank, in this case 2.5 metres wide. And in those two years he has found 2,070 species. This is very much an underestimate, as many taxonomic groups have not been thoroughly sampled.[14]

Robert Walton was well aware of how much he was missing. He did not include either the tawny owl or the sparrowhawk, both of which visit the farm and will inevitably have visited the hedge. And while Robert scored an impressive 56 species of fungi, Georg Muller once found 280 species in a single hedge bank.

Walton clearly manages his land with wildlife in mind,

and he has ensured that his hedge is complete with 'shrubs, emergent trees, bank, ditch and herbaceous margins.' This provides a myriad microclimates – the only thing lacking, in his estimation, is a couple of mature trees. He manages the hedge with care. It was last laid in 1999/2000, and is cut with a flail every three to four years to keep it thick and bushy. Eventually it will start to grow out and need laying again, which he admits is, 'an expensive and time-consuming business', especially as he has over 9 kilometres of hedge on his land.

The advantage he has is that it is an old hedge. A fascinating feature of hedges has been formulated into 'Hooper's Rule', named after Dr Max Hooper, who counted the number of tree and woody-shrub species in 227 hedges of known age, and found a great deal of correlation between the number of species and the age of the hedge. As a rule of thumb, the number of species found in a 30-metre sample stretch is equivalent to the number of centuries the hedge has been there.[15]

Oliver Rackham presents a number of detailed exceptions to the Rule, and considers potential explanations, including the simple notion that as hedges age they accumulate more species. However, he makes the point that hedges planted during the enclosures tended to contain fewer species, while those planted beforehand had a wider range of species, probably depending on what was available locally. A Bristol University study, meanwhile, has shown how the 'majority of biodiversity on a Somerset farm could be conserved by retaining and appropriately managing uncultivated habitats such as hedges. The importance of hedges and "waste ground" for maintaining overall ecological integrity was out of all proportion to the 4.5 per cent of the land area which they occupied.'[16] In other words, hedges are a valuable conservation refuge. They are key to allowing the natural world a little more space, linking larger sites of wildlife value, whether nature reserves or SSSIs, into what is becoming recognised as a 'Living Landscape'. Without one of the most important contributors to the biodiversity of our land, therefore, the few pockets of wildlife habitat remaining to us would be isolated islands surrounded by a barren and sometimes toxic sea of industry. I just hope that hedges can survive another century or two to enable the ecologists of the future to see if Hooper's Rule really holds true.

But there is also what the hedge gives to us. Originally hedges were there to protect us from the wild; now they link us to the wild. A walk along a hedge is never wasted. The eternal clock of life ticks on through the changes of colour, the shifting scents and stirring sounds. Go in the evening and see it wake up as a highway. Bats use them not only to feed over and live in (if there are mature trees with inviting holes), but also to travel along. Stop and listen as the small mammals that have hidden in the day away from sharp eyes and sharper talons begin their commute, not quite as out of reach to us as the squeaks of bats; the mice, voles and shrews are audible even to my ears. Toads I imagine stepping across the threshold of their daytime shelter and surveying the scene with a proprietorial air. Moths, food for so many, flicker awake and take to the wing, driven by their own spectrum of smell to feed and mate. Larger residents assert their ownership of the line, through foxes' quick stink and badgers' barrelling run. A tawny owl views all such activity with possible disdain, just waiting for a vole to veer into view.

A hedge is connection – for wildlife, of course, but also for us. It is along the hedges that the green lanes run, and that those edge-dwellers find a home. Not just the hedgehogs, but also people who want to straddle the worlds of the civilised and the pagan. Like many, I imagine, I find the constraints of urban life sometimes just too much – and the hedgerows are places to dip a toe into wild waters without risk of being swept away.

3

Ditches and Dykes

We are prone to thinking in a human timescale. We look at our landscape and imagine that this is what it is. But if we extend our timelines it is clear that we live on shifting sands. For example, the Thames estuary is sinking at around a foot each century, and Scotland is rearing up.

Change is always happening, and sometimes we cause that change. We humans have the capacity to create habitable land, and in so doing create new and amazing habitats for wildlife as well. Of course, that also comes with an ecological cost as wetlands are lost.

About a quarter of the British Isles is or was some kind of wetland. The fluctuations of the water levels reflect changes in the ice sheets of Antarctica and Greenland. There have been times when it was higher – in the Bronze Age, for example. Today we are in the middle of a global experiment to see what happens when there is a dramatic change in sea-level. As the climate changes and temperatures rise, so the ice sheets begin to retreat, releasing stored water and increasing the risk to all coastal communities, which include the world's most densely populated.

That is all still to come, and will need some imaginative

solutions to prevent catastrophe. Looking back in time we can see that the management of water levels has been a crucial component of our growth. There are great drains, as substantial as industrial canals, that keep the Somerset Levels drier than they might be. But it is wrong to think of this as just the work of Sir Cornelius Vermuyden, spreading the lessons learned in the Netherlands and 'reclaiming' the Fens in the seventeenth century. Dutch ditches and dykes are famous lines that have helped create a country.

In Britain, first came the work of the Romans, and then another tranche of trenching in the thirteenth century. And while the aim was usually to create land by draining water away, this was also a time of destruction and disenfranchisement. Commonly-owned wetlands that supplied small communities with food were drained and enclosed.

An example of these enclosures comes from close to home. Otmoor, just outside Oxford, was a marsh that flooded regularly, used communally by the communities living around its edge. In 1815 an Enclosure Act was signed, handing the land over to the wealthy landowners and causing, in reaction, civil unrest. The riots in 1829–30 have made it into folk history and folk song. In 'Otmoor Forever', by the dark and crafty musicians of the band Telling the Bees, the tale is richly told, concluding with the gloomy couplet, 'We won the battle but we lost the war/ Because none of us works the land no more.' The drive to drain and enclose the land came in part from plants that originated in the Middle East, like wheat, barley and flax. These crops do not take kindly to inundation.

Another line threatened Otmoor in the 1980s, when it was decided that the M40 should take the most direct route – across this historic landscape. Campaigners fought to halt the process, employing an ingenious scheme of encouraging people to buy fragments of one particular field, making the process of compulsory purchase far harder. The division of 'Alice's Meadow', so named after the pattern of hedges, ditches and dykes on Otmoor that partly inspired the chessboard in Lewis Carroll's *Through the Looking-Glass*, into 3,500 individual plots was a major factor in the motorway being forced to bypass Otmoor. Now the moor is most famous for its wildlife, and in particular as a brilliant place to watch murmurations: swarming shoals of starlings using the hedge- and treelines for communal roosting.

We have always been altering the landscape. Changes for good or ill might last a lifetime, or more, but for the land they transform they are just brief moments. So what we have at present is a mere snapshot in time, of something that used to be different and will be different again. With this in mind it is worth looking afresh at the ditches and dykes that weave and stride around the country.

Ditches are always going to be associated with dykes. In part the association is semantic: they are both rooted in the same word, *dik* in Middle English, *diki* in Old Norse. Partly it is a question of place – in the north of Britain what is called a dyke is what in the south is often called a ditch. And it is also down to the simple reality that when you dig a ditch you need to deposit the soil, and you often do that in the form of a dyke.

Some are large, some small; some have a dramatic impact on the land; others, well, are hardly noticed until something goes wrong. Many are easily missed, as they accompany hedges in their travels; in many parts of the country they are a field margin, harbouring a flourishing variety of life that remains largely out of sight and out of mind. Such moist corridors must, to the resident fauna, seem as endless and awesome as the Amazon is to us. When inundated, however, they can turn into streams, known in some parts of Britain as 'running dykes'.

All over the world ditches, dykes and drains have been key in the reclamation of land. They can be for protecting newly created land, or conversely for the prevention of land being created. The soft coasts of these islands are at the mercy of the sea, and there are many instances of loss as the coast-line has retreated inland. And while billions of pounds have been spent trying to shore up the shoreline, pragmatism has also kicked in, with 'managed retreat' often now considered the best option. On my visits to west Dorset over the years I have been amazed at how the coastline has changed. The cliffs take periodic crumbles into the ocean, revealing a tantalising, if rather risky to reach, tumble of fossils. The coastline around Lyme Regis is held together like Evil Knievel's skeleton, pinned against the forces of water and gravity.

These forces are central to the work of the Great Fen Project – an ambitious plan to reclaim 3,700 hectares of some of the country's most fertile farmland between Peterborough and Huntingdon and return it to the wild. This is a land-scape already under heavy pressure from new housing developments, but the project has managed to raise considerable funds on the back of a fifty-year plan and has already secured over half of the land on its wish list.

Since the seventeenth century the wild fens that once stretched for hundreds of miles have been transformed, drained and managed. Culverts, ditches and drains have been engineered into a brilliantly designed lattice, eradicating around 99 per cent of this once-dominant wetland habitat. Two of the patches of original fen left, Woodwalton Fen and Holme Fen, are National Nature Reserves and within a couple of kilometres of each other. Inspired, therefore, by Sir John Lawton's principles of 'bigger, better and more joined-up', the Great Fen Project was born to reconnect these two beautiful examples of a very rare habitat. To do this, the project's team are building new drains with very different purposes. Lines were once the nemesis of this fenland, taking the water away. Now, new linear features are going to bring back the lifeblood of this land. The project's Restoration Officer is Helen Bailey, who radiates a passion for her work, so I arranged to visit her on site.

Following a long drive from Oxford I came to the green barn she had told me to look out for near a small plantation of conifers. There was a rough track to the left. As I pulled in, I could see Helen and her colleague Mark Ullyett, the Restoration Manager, sitting outside on logs drinking tea, despite the rather grey May morning.

As I stretched myself out of the car I was greeted by something so special and rare I had to think for a moment what it was, so wrapped up had I been in the troubles of the world.

There it was again: *cuck-oo, cuck-oo* – the minor third of spring. First of the year. And over that? The great space of quiet, just long enough to register before we said hello and settled down to business. As I joined them on one of the rough-hewn seats with a mug of restorative tea, I noticed the cuckoo had been drowned out by skylarks. Little gladdens my heart more than the tumbling beauty of sky-lark song.

Helen and Mark appeared deeply contented souls, and spending a day travelling around their patch with them it would become obvious why. Their work was rewarding, and their working environment just as inspiring. The big sky overhead dissolved any tension I felt as thoroughly as a mas-sage. But most important of all they were making a tangible difference; what they were doing was creating change.

We were right next to what was once England's second largest lake, Whittlesea Mere. As we pored over maps I was reminded once more of the short timeframes we operate in. By 1851, when the Mere was finally drained, it was already much reduced in size, but the late-seventeenth-century traveller Celia Fiennes referred to it being 'three mile broad and six mile long'.

The motivations for draining it are obvious: it enabled the railways to be built, and it released fertile land into the farm-ing system. At that time, however, there would have been some sense of balance between farming and nature – farming was much more a part of the natural world than it is now. But efficiency is the killer, and over the years efficiency has spread into every corner of the farming world, and extirpated so much above and below ground, to create deserts coated in a wash of green.

Mark Ullyett, who comes from farming stock and knows the land, had an interesting insight into this. 'People who live on the land,' he said, 'have a very different psychology. They want to hand it on in a better condition. But now so much of the work is done by contractors who are not connected to the land – they work with a detachment that allows them to do things their predecessors would not have done. The drive for efficiency has removed the idea of husbandry.'

Of course, food needs to be produced, but the true cost of removing nature from the equation is, I fear, something we are now beginning to realise. On top of this there are new pressures on this precious land: the communities of Cambridge and Peterborough are both expanding, putting more of the green under grey. So linking two of the remaining bits of wild fen will at least help to provide a redoubt against the siege engines of efficiency and progress.

But this project is a mad scheme, I objected – there are farms in the way! What farmer is going to give up their land for flooding?

'This is not a short-term project,' Helen said. 'I doubt many of us will be alive when we get to the end of the fifty-year plan. And we do understand that giving up land is difficult for farmers. But we started in 2001, and already we have over 55 per cent ownership.' This is not about kicking farmers off the land, I was assured – the Crown rents much of this land out, and tenants have a three-generation lease, so time is necessary before the tenancy can become available.

Break-time over, and I noticed the skylarks had been replaced by chattering swallows and a charm of goldfinches. It is a long time since I have spent time in such a clearly rich, yet heavily farmed environment. The potential transform-ation of the landscape it hinted at was exciting.

I was given the front seat of the project Land Rover, and as we bounced off I remarked on how well this project must fit the 'rewilding' agenda popularised by George Monbiot – that we can bring great benefits in biodiversity by simply stepping back and allowing nature to work its own magic.

'You are missing the point,' said Helen. 'This is not rewild-ing. We are controlling the process, and it is a process that can be undone should situations change. Though that does not mean it is any less important.' She pulled up beside a long straight ditch running perpendicular to the track. It was part of the system run by the Internal Drainage Board, the operat-ing authority empowered by the Land Drainage Act of 1991. 'You can always tell if it is one of theirs,' she said. 'They tend to be straight, steep and flailed. We are just waiting until they are happy for us to let this area become a little wetter.'

A little further on we pulled in next to some charred tree stumps. How odd, I commented, to have a collection of partly burnt trees acting as a very porous fence.

'You have not come across "bog oak", I guess,' said Mark. 'These, and there are countless still to find, are the relics of the forest that used to blanket this area. As the water rose, they died and sank into what became a very peaty mire which preserved them. These could be thousands of years old. And as the peat retreats, so they re-emerge.' Bog oak – or bog wood; it does not have to be oak – is at the first stages of fossilisation. Given enough time it would become coal. For now it is a nuisance to the farmers, whose ploughs are used to softer substrate.

Between the bog wood pillars, with a woodland of silver birch beyond, was a large and uneventful field of grass. That was how it seemed to me, at least, but to Mark and Helen it was an exciting patch of land. This was where the process of reclamation that would eventually lead to new lines being cut to re-wet this drained landscape was starting. Just two years earlier this field was still producing onions. Now it had been seeded with a special mix of grass to provide food for returning wildlife and also begin the process of removing nutrients from the soil.

But wasn't the point of these fields that they grew such fine crops because the soil was so rich? At my feet was a fantastic molehill – I could not resist sinking my hands into the rich brown soil that the velvety beast had pushed up to the surface. Such a sensual delight – the structure of the soil was so light that little effort was required to get in deep, and the handful I emerged with ran between my fingers like sand. I did it again, so good had it felt.

Helen was smiling at my fascination. 'The soil here is an amazing substrate,' she agreed. 'Root crops were a favourite, as you could pull them up pretty much clean, and they grew true in the friable soil. But they long since used up the natural capacity of the soil to cause life to flourish. Now they are supported by the agricultural equivalent of Viagra – the artificial fertilisers that prevent wild plants returning.' It is one of those ecological puzzles I need to get my head around. Intellectually I know that to create a wild flower meadow you need poor-quality soil. But my brain is hard-wired to the logic that says a rich array of plant life must come from rich nutrients.

The trouble with a field rich in nutrients is that it attracts plants that thrive in that environment, and such plants crowd out the opposition. Which is exactly what farmers need. They need the field to be full of nothing but their crop, so they manage the land to discourage competition. Failing that, they blast it into the netherworld with an arsenal of agrotoxins. But even then there is no guarantee of success – later that day we passed a small mountain of rotting potatoes. 'Probably the wrong size for the contract,' said Helen. 'There are times that the air is thick with the smell of decaying onions that were just not quite right – they just get left to rot. There is a madness in the food chain that allows such nonsense.'

To start the process of reconnection the project has the fields ploughed and rolled, and seeded with grass mix. The results of that are what I saw, and they are not overwhelming. But they are the beginning, and an essential one. If the land were left bare it would quickly be hit by 'fen blow'. I had not come across this term before. Mark explained how the fens suffer when the fields are left exposed: winds can whip up the topsoil into a wall of dust that makes driving treacherous – 'like driving through Marmite,' said one poor motorist quoted by the BBC. (It would have to be a peculiarly dusty and rather spiderwebby sort of Marmite, a friend who knows the area pointed out.) Whatever its texture, fen blow is a serious problem, robbing the land of the soil needed to support new growth. So the grass is planted to bind it together while the seeds and moisture work their magic.

The grass is then cropped as hay, creating good-quality feed for livestock. Next, sheep will be introduced, and as they will select the coarser grass to eat, that will allow wildflowers to emerge. Soon the field will become tussocky, just the sort of landscape farmers would be trying to avoid. And by then the wildlife will be starting to move back in. Small mammals love rough pasture; owls and other birds of prey love small mammals. Meadow pipits and corn buntings nest in among the tussocks too, feeding in the shorter grass.

The final stage of the process requires a choice to be made: whether a field should be left fairly dry, so that it will evolve into scrub, birch woodland and eventually more substantial trees; or whether water levels should be allowed to rise.

'Later we'll show you where we've been preparing the ground to be wetter,' Mark said. 'But now, come and see this.' We went on a little further, walking parallel to the narrow but sporadically very busy road.

The road was slightly raised, by less than a metre, I guess, but enough to present any reclamation scheme with a problem. Water would need to be flooding to cross this barrier. If the project was about rewilding then the road would just go, but this landscape will remain populated, and people need access. This is where an instrument called a thrust borer comes into its own. Either side of the road, ditches accumulated water and, though that water looked pretty still, it remained inexorably susceptible to the law of gravity. Two large holes acted as drains and sinks for the water, and now a tunnel had been bored to connect them. Not cheap, but an example of how to work with the land but also not against the people who live there.

As we drove on I began to notice the life in the bank separating us from the newly grassed field: hemlock, mallow, white dead nettles, burdock, dandelions and spear thistle. Nothing outrageous, nothing to attract the botanical twitchers, but nevertheless, a beginning, one that the scratchy whitethroat was clearly enjoying, even if, as always, it sounded a little grumpy. I could imagine this margin soon being swamped in butterflies.

The whole landscape felt as though it was being managed in some middle way between the carefree rewilding that removes humans from the equation altogether and the species-specific focus of organisations like the RSPB. And while I still balk a little at anything that reminds me of the Blairite Third Way, it is possible that taking a managed approach to reclaiming land might be more practical than rewilding and far more useful than dipping it in ecological aspic for the benefit of a very few species.

Now Helen was pointing out of the window with the air of a tour guide. 'Here we have the lowest point in Britain – three metres below sea level.' I should have asked for us to stop, but we were on our way to something more exciting. We were heading to the Holme Posts.

Mark began to tell me the story. 'Back in 1848, when the drainage of Whittlesea Mere was begun in earnest, William Wells, a local landowner, decided to see how much the ground would subside. So he drove an oak pole through the peat until it became embedded in the clay below, and cut the top off so it lay flush with the ground. A few years later a metal version was installed, and the true extent of how much we have sunk – well, you will see in a minute.'

With that we pulled into a layby. I got Helen to stand beside one of the two tall metal poles rising up out of the ground. It was three times her height – over 4 metres high. That was how much the land had receded since draining began.

The ditch that ran beside the posts was another of the Internal Drainage Board ditches, straight as a Roman road, a line that let water linger, but inexorably pulled it from the land. And it was lined by cuckoo flower, or lady's smock, pretty and delicate in a way the ditch wasn't.

Back in the Land Rover Mark pointed out the fields to our left, which had patches of mud showing through the grass. These were, he said, 'scrapes' – heavy machinery had been brought in to scrape shallow hollows, so that when water levels rose, as new ditches brought water back to this dry land, there would be enough contour in the once bowling-green-flat fields to allow temporary ponds to form.

I am a big fan of the ephemeral pond. All over the country there are dips that become, even for just a few days, bodies of water of great importance to wildlife. And it is wonderful how swiftly these ponds fill up with life, whether it has lain dormant in the soil, blown in on the wind or paddled there on the feet of ducks.

So quickly have the worked areas of the Great Fen Project improved for wildlife that there had been the first incidence of confrontation with the local farming community. The number of little owls had reached a point where they were attracting crowds of birders, who were using passing-places on the narrow lanes to park in. This, sadly, was not going to persuade the locals of the value of wildlife.

Which leads us on to a question still unanswered. What is being created here: something for wildlife, or something for people?

Going some way to resolve this conundrum was the latest bird hide, raised off the ground and left unlocked, though it had to be kept shut, otherwise owls took up residence and made a mess, evidence of which was clearly visible. The view was restful, if a little uneventful, but again this was just the start. What we were looking out on was the result of the subtle application of large machinery. What was once a square reservoir for the farmer had now been softened, with banks less steep and the sides rounder. Mark pointed out the other scraping that had been done, with ditches slubbed out, creating what is now known as Ryme's Reedbed. But this partial dredging was not all. The most important thing was the new ditches, 3 kilometres of meandering waterway to help the fen managers to keep water levels optimal. The measurement was more sophisticated than just looking into the ditches: small boxes, dip wells, were scattered around the site from which data was being gathered on the depth. Walking back to the car I could hear evidence of success: a sedge warbler, scratchy and percussive, declaring ownership.

On our meandering route back to base we drove along narrow tracks between fields just beginning to show evidence of the work already done. I started to picture a landscape teaming in wildlife: reeds would grow, water would predominate. The rattle of warblers would become common. 'A hare!' shouted Helen. And there it was, regarding us with little concern before turning and loping off: more evidence of the changing biodiversity of this landscape, sculpted by line. I had not seen a hare for a year or so. Pictures in books do no justice to the magic of these animals. Rabbits are like a domesticated, infantilised version of the hare; the real thing carries authority, grace and beauty.

Why, I asked, were some of these obviously quite old roads gently curving? It was not as if they were following the field margins laid down by the chaotic collection of immovable hedges – these roads could run as straight as they wanted. Well, it turned out that many fen roads follow old riverbeds, so they do have an organic origin: in the riverbeds clay has collected, which is a far more substantial foundation for the transport network.

The lines we imposed on this landscape over the last few centuries are being remodelled to flood, and new ditches are being dug that will restore water to these historically boggy fields. The linescape will create a massive change, and I relish the thought of returning, though by the time the project is complete it is probable that none of us, Helen, Mark or I, will be around to experience the return of the wild to the Great Fen.

*

Some dykes are of a rather grander scale than those being used to drain and train the wetter lands. Perhaps the most famous was built by Offa, king of Mercia from 757 to 796, to defend his land from invasion by the neighbouring kingdom of Powys. While we know it was up to 20 metres wide and over 2 metres high, the original length of the dyke is still debated, with some arguing that it ran for 240 kilometres from sea to sea, from the River Dee in the north to the River Wye in the south. But the earthworks don't exist to back this up. The official figure for this martial barrier is nearly 130 kilometres. Now, though, it has a far gentler purpose, as part of one of the longest National Trails, stretching for 283 kilometres from the Severn Estuary to Prestatyn in North Wales.

I had the opportunity to link up with Rob Dingle, the Offa's Dyke Trail Officer. Rob has one of the best jobs – as long as he can keep out of the office, that is. We met in a café in Kington in Herefordshire, an old, small and largely closed market town. There is little more tantalising than walking by an exceptionally lovely-looking secondhand bookshop, with books I wanted in the window, and finding that Wednesday afternoons are just not for opening. One day I will return to Kington, but not on a Wednesday.

Rob had just got back from guiding a walk on the Trail and, as with so many people I met while researching these lines, he brimmed with enthusiasm for his work and his world. He understood my fascination with lines right away. 'The great thing about this dyke is that it is really well protected,' he said. 'It is a Scheduled Ancient Monument, which means it is legally protected from damage and destruction. So it can't be cultivated. Also, it is a long ridge, so it is pretty difficult to cultivate anyway. And this means we have got a long, linear nature reserve that is 1,250 years old and filled with some gorgeous veteran trees.'

It is not perfectly protected, of course. A 50-metre section of the monument at Chirk, near Wrexham in north Wales, was bulldozed in 2013, yet the man who did it managed to escape sanction by claiming to be unaware of the monument. At the time Rob had been horrified, indeed, he had been reported in the press describing it as 'one of the worst examples of direct damage to the monument that I've heard about', but he had an enviably positive spirit and was now managing to find some positives in the destruction. The unsubtle excavation gave archaeologists a chance to probe around and find, with carbon dating, that this section of the Dyke was up to 400 years older than had been thought. 'This means that Offa might not have just built the Dyke as a single entity, but also included older structures along the way.'

'So much of the Dyke has been lost in a piecemeal fashion,' Rob explained as he drove us out to the Dyke, 'either through ignorance, like the person up in Chirk, or deliberately. And we only got protection on this monument in 1979, so before that, who knows. While the Trail is 177 miles long, the Dyke is 80 miles – still the longest archaeological ancient monument in Britain.' He is rather pleased to point out that Hadrian's Wall is only 73 miles long. 'I look at this Dyke as a thread that joins together a series of gems,' he said as we pulled in to park. 'All the way along there are castles, hill forts, nature reserves and stunning views.'

We walked up from the road and in front of me there was a rather unimpressive tree-lined bump. Oilseed rape to my left, sheep to my right, and in the middle a vague hint at a path through a bed of nettles. We were both in shorts, but this did nothing to dampen Rob's enthusiasm, so I braced myself and followed him into the sea of sting. Swiftly I was reminded of a wonderful word: 'urtification'. The Latin for the stinging nettle is *Urtica dioica*, and urtification is the use of these well-defended plants to relieve rheumatism, arthritis, gout and tendonitis. Apparently Roman legionaries would beat their legs with nettles to relieve the pain of long marches. Suffering, as I do, from an irritating multitude of joint-based ailments, I was intrigued by how quickly the stinging sub-sided into a background glow that was far from unpleasant. So it remained for most of the rest of the day.

Soon the ground to my right began to fall away, but the Dyke still seemed a little unimpressive. 'Ignore what you see to the left,' Rob explained. 'That is the east. The Dyke was built to deter the Welsh, so you will see all along its length the ditch is always to the west. It did not matter that the Mercians could not see it: it was not for them.'

But even so, unless this was once heavily fortified with thousands of guards, it hardly presented much of an obstacle for marauders. Was it just very heavily eroded? 'You are miss-ing the point of the Dyke,' Rob said. 'It was largely psychological. It was a statement. If you are out on a walk and you come across a string of barbed wire with a sign say-ing "Keep out", you tend to abide by the injunction. The story was spread that any Welshman found on the wrong side of the Dyke would be vigorously returned, minus an ear. This was a symbol of power.'

Much of the power has been undermined now, and there are two main problems that this line faces. Deliberate destruction, as in the bulldozing incident, is rare. But there is a subtler war of attrition going on, as the incremental damage caused by the furrow from the plough edges closer year on year. The ecological value of the line is supported by its boundaries, and in many places this 3–4-metre margin has been eroded. As we emerged from the bed of tingling nettles it became clear that here it was not the plough that was encroaching, but sheep. There was enough snared wool on the hawthorns to make a jumper or two.

The other agent of doom comes in more natural form. 'Can you imagine a more attractive proposition for a badger?' Rob said. 'Eighty miles of raised, well-drained land – this is badger heaven. And here, you can see what they can do.' We were on top of the Dyke with the rape to our left and a wire fence to the right, under which a clear badger track led to a sett, complete with freshly cleared bedding dragged into the field, and a rubble of soil and stone fanning from the front door.

Badgers get blamed for a lot of things that are not necessarily their fault. But here on Offa's Dyke it really seemed the blame was just, if understandable. The worst damage, it turned out, was caused not by badgers alone, but by the badgers creating tunnels underneath sections of Dyke frequented by cattle. This was what caused collapses. We have created a topography that could not be more natural for badgers, and they are using it as ignorant of the history being disturbed as the bloke up in Chirk. What to do? It would be impossible to exclude them from the entire length of the Dyke.

Beyond the hawthorns and badger setts, this section of the Dyke was beginning to show some promise. We stopped and looked west. 'That is the Walton Basin,' said Rob. I could see why he had chosen this spot. It looked a little like a vision from a geography textbook displaying a glacial landscape. The rounded hills once held Roman encampments, and before that Neolithic and Bronze Age settlements. Now they were covered with sheep and other agriculture. And above us, oak trees, some properly old examples, venerable and warped by time. 'These are the "veterans" I was talking about. Some of these must be well over 300 years old now, and just look,' he said, pointing along the line: 'there is almost continual tree canopy from the woodland where we left the car to the copse on ahead. And all along the Dyke there are protected lines like this, trees that have been allowed to show some of their potential, growing in a protected space.'

These beautiful trees are not without cost, however. They are eating into the Dyke, and where the soil is heavily eroded by sheep – who use this tree line for shelter – there is always the risk of a storm bringing a majestic oak down, lifting with its root plate a great hole from the bank.

This section of the Dyke, at least, is a wonderful example of inadvertent wildlife management. The aim has been to maintain the archaeological and historical integrity of the site, but the benefits to wildlife are plenty. And the changes wrought by history have also added to the good: Rob pointed out how beside the dug-out ditch segment below, a green lane had also been created, as needy feet found a line along which to walk.

As we headed back along the Dyke to Rob's car I could not help but envy a life spent walking this one line. Rob has his patch, but it is such a long patch that by the time he returns to any one section, so much will have changed. Even now, as the rain was falling on us in an invisibly fine drizzle, it was wonderful. Ravens cronked, nettles stimulated and the oaks stood. 'You do realise that three-quarters of my life is spent in the office,' Rob said, rather bursting my bubble. 'I have to organise the management of this Trail, though I wish I could be out every day.' So we were doing each other a favour. I was giving him good cause to avoid paperwork, phones and computers for another day, and he was showing me part of our nation's linescape. While it once defended Mercia from the wild people of Powys, now it protects oak trees and their lichens, offering jewels, natural and archaeological, along a line that would have been subsumed into agriculture had Offa been less territorial. And as with all these lines, the wildlife benefit was not their reason for existing. It is just good fortune and good management that gifts us this prize.

Ditches and dykes have been integral to the changes in Britain, reclaiming land, protecting land and returning land to nature. Canals are coming soon, but for now we move on to walls.

4

Walls

North Ronaldsay, small, flat and most northerly of the Orkneys, has a famous 2-metre-high perimeter wall. Which is,
rather confusingly, referred to as the 'dyke'. At 12 miles it is
probably the longest dry-stone wall, conceived as a single
piece of work, anywhere in the world. And it has a very
important job. Not repelling Viking raiders (they made
themselves at home centuries ago), but keeping sheep on the
beach, where they have evolved an unusual diet, one rich in
seaweed.

Before it was built in 1832 the sheep had the run of the
island, and the islanders made their living from the plentiful
kelp growing in the cold clear waters. Kelp was first and
foremost a fertiliser for the fields, but by the 18th century a
new use had been discovered. Kelp was crucial to the chemical industry as a source of iodine and alkali. This alga was
collected and stacked to dry in the wind before the summer
burn, which reduced the weed to ash. To produce a ton of
this chemical-rich ash required 20 tons of seaweed, and in a
good year the island could produce 100 tons of processed
weed. The manufacturers of glass and soap relied upon this
hard work.

But with the emergence of more cheaply sourced chemicals from South America, demand slackened, until in the 1930s burning ceased altogether. However, kelp, or tangles as it is known, is still harvested to this day, but now the product sought is alginate – alginic acid – a highly absorbent polysaccharide used as a thickener in drinks and ice cream, as a gelling agent and in pharmaceuticals such as antacids. But kelp is no longer crucial to the island's economy, so the islanders can afford to let the sheep feast on it. So acclimatised are they to this strange diet that sheep moved onto permanent pasture have succumbed to copper poisoning.

Maintenance of this mighty wall was based on need, with labour provided in proportion to the number of sheep in your household's allocation. Over the years I have spent quite some time on this island, initially counting hedgehogs, and however much you might think you own the sheep, in my experience they had ideas of their own. Sheep have their own tribes, known as 'clowgangs', which brook no incursions from other sheep and will 'doose' them – a swift head-to-head communication.

The wall on North Ronaldsay had another role, for me at least, as a line that I could cross when I needed to escape. Inside it was humanity: grass managed by blade and cow, homes, roads, shops and, on more than one occasion, a complicated relationship. Outside the wall, in particular to the west, was wildness. I would go to the rocks and sit and feel the surging power of the ocean. Looking out to sea it was easy to imagine my line of sight grazing the southern tip of Greenland before hitting Newfoundland. Separated by a line of rocks were two very different worlds. Mark Cocker, another writer captivated by this eccentric island, described this line perfectly in his blog: 'the dyke is compelling because it marks the point of transition from the human to the natural, from cultural to the wild. Inshore are the grazing pastures and the beautiful stonework of the ancient crofts and now the wind turbines and the people. Beyond the dyke is a landscape every bit as wild and untrammelled and as self-renewing as a rainforest.'[1]

Its stonework is never just grey. Lichen, a dusty palette from pale to yellow and orange, sits and waits and slowly grows. It is a contented organism: there is no rush or stress; it can grow imperceptibly. Maybe this comes from the calmness required to work symbiotically – to have two very different life forms weaving their needs together and creating something so much greater than the sum of their parts. Millions of years of negotiation between fungus and alga have allowed them to reach a point of evolutionary Nirvana.

With wonderful connectivity lichen was scraped from the stones and used to dye the wool from the sheep. A lichen called crotal, for example, was at the heart of the Harris tweed industry, generating a ruddy brown colour. So important was lichen, indeed, that the saying went, 'Cattle on the hills, gold on the stones.' Currently there is no dyeing of wool on North Ronaldsay, mainly because the wool comes in such a rich array of colours without extra help. Though the yarn collective on the island told me that they had a visitor from Denmark who used green lichen to dye the wool a nice purple colour.

The wall is home to so much more than the spattering of lichen. Black guillemots, known on the islands as 'tysties', are handsome black birds that flash a white wing patch and, when feeling daring, reveal a little bit of their bright red leg. Some make use of this artificial cliff, nesting in the interstices.

Beside the wall nests the fulmar, the most beautiful of birds – beautiful to look at, that is, but a foul fowl in manner. The mollymawk (most birds have different names up here) is the doe-eyed relative of the albatross, the gliding angel that effortlessly surfs the waves of air above the churning sea, and then makes for home back by the wall, to look out, and wait, and incubate. Its natural home is the cliff, and the wall provides a substantial analogue, albeit a little less lift. But as the air is rarely still, flight comes easily.

While the wall can act as a sanctuary for the fulmar, however, there is a darker side. There is more wall to the island than just a perimeter boundary – there are a series of punds, small walled fields, into which the sheep are encouraged for shearing and castration. These punds have become unexpected hazards for the fulmar. Their gregarious nature encourages them to accumulate – if something is good enough for one it must be good enough for all. Unfortunately, in summer the punds become a death-trap. Nettles and other vegetation take advantage of the great fertility left behind by nervous sheep. This alone is not a problem, but when you get a collision of rain, no wind and a curious fulmar, the problems begin. In such a place a wet and bedraggled fulmar will struggle to take to the wing: no chance of a run-up; no wind to provide lift – and the more it struggles the more the smell (and trust me, fulmars have a very distinctive and quite projectile scent) gets spread around, and the more other fulmars get the idea that this must be a great place to be. Hundreds of fulmars have been rescued from starvation in these punds by the ornithologists from North Ronaldsay's wonderful bird observatory. I have helped and, for my efforts, been bitten and vomited on by these vile, beautiful creatures.

Winter storms come in from the Atlantic, the North Sea and the Arctic and cause damage that needs repair. Like the island itself, the wall around it is at risk. Great storms in 2012 broke the siege of nearly 200 years – a war of attrition that gained this victory thanks possibly to climate change, but definitely the loss of people. When I was first on North Ronaldsay in the mid-1980s there were over ninety inhabitants; now there are fewer than fifty. The wall was built when there were nearer 500. The availability of work is at the heart of it – there is nothing to compare with the lure of the Orkney mainland (after a few months on the island the bustle of Kirkwall takes you by surprise), and then Scotland, and then the world. But still North Ronaldsay lures ornithologists. And could, should its mind be turned that way, entice those who crave the isolation, the wild peace of a place where the mind can wander. Art can happen in a place like this. There is no surprise that the archipelago has sprung such wonder on the world: George Mackay Brown, Edwin Muir and, though not a native, the deeply missed Peter Maxwell Davies.

Now the wall is maintained by whoever has the time and energy. When I last enquired, it was down to one man who was spending what spare time he had rebuilding the defences, which means more than simply placing rocks on top of one another. There is as much art involved as science and engineering. I once tried to help, only to discover that my effort had been so appalling it had to be taken down and done again.

*

Walls like this are obviously not restricted to the furthest reaches of Britain, and are second only to hedges as a defining landscape feature – indeed, in some parts of the country they are easily the most definite. There are line-managers who have dedicated their lives to looking after these peculiarly organic lines of inorganic matter. My search for someone who combined the profound skill of making walls with a knowledge of what other life depends on them led me to Trevor Wragg, and his home in the Derbyshire Peak District, right in the heart of the stonewall world, in the almost too cute village of Hartington.

The drive there, across the plain, or more likely plateau, on which the Roman road had laser-etched its path, was testament to the power of geology, as rock and stone were everywhere. My reading on walls now made me aware of things that needed explaining. Why in that large field (surrounded by dry-stone wall, of course) was there at its centre a small clump of ash trees surrounded by a circle of wall – was it an Andy Goldsworthy installation? Why was there a line of sycamores growing in a long and very narrow field, surrounded by long walls? So much effort put in to stopping those trees escaping. I am not very good at drawing, but I was moved to stop and park up and hamfistedly try to capture something of what I saw. Then in the middle distance there was a hill that two thirds of the way up had a wall running all the way around it. That, I surmised, probably marked the limit of the worthwhile grazing, but then I could see a series of elegant arcs of wall sweeping down the hill in gentle and clearly deliberate curves. Why not straight? I've seen straight walls heading downhill, so it is not impossible. And on the steep hillside on the approach to Hartington there was what appeared to be a retaining wall, a 20-metre arc of dry-stone wall.

Trevor was full of energy and enthusiasm, mischief and gentle self-confidence. As a good ice-breaker I decided I would start by asking him all the questions that had been bubbling away during the journey. First, those circular walls: what were they for?

'I know you are here to learn about lines,' he said, starting what was to become a standard and cryptic style of answer. 'But you are forgetting that there are lines underground, lines that brought so many people out here.' That was it: seams, mining seams. 'Lead drew people up here and they sank shafts. Most of the mining stopped in the nineteenth century, but the shafts remained as a reminder and a hazard, so people built walls around them. In other places there are stone or concrete covers – some look like beehives – but that was actually a mine shaft. And the trees – well, livestock was not

85

going to get in there, so the trees were free to grow. Sometimes they are not entrances, though, but sink holes. They can open up after really wet weather and swallow whatever is unfortunate to be above it. I have seen cars half-submerged in the land.'

During the seventeenth century lead mining was second only to wool in economic importance to the country. There are hundreds of miles of tunnels through the Peak District. These tunnels have had unexpected consequences, revealing some of the deepest and most impressive natural caves.

Lead mining has left other, more visible lines. Veins of ore have been uncovered, initially through time eroding the stone above the relics of Carboniferous volcanoes to bring the solidified, mineral-rich magma closer to the surface, and subsequently with expertise, picks, and shovels. Those veins, known as 'rakes,' that are near the surface can be traced for miles by ridge-like spoil banks. Sometimes these have an attendant treeline, planted, and then protected by walls, to keep livestock from grazing the potentially poisonous land.[2]

Though not all lines of trees protected by walls are to do with rakes. The ones I had noted on the way to meet Trevor had a different purpose. 'What have we got more of up here than lead and stone?' he asked. He glanced up into the bright blue sky above Hartington, and even on such a day I was struck by the play the jackdaws were making up in it. Wind. I could see how the trees made a shelter belt, but why the walls?

'Up here trees are very valuable. They gave us fuel,

building material and, as you guessed, shelter for the sheep. Why are there so few trees up here? Because of the sheep. The walls were built from something there is lots of, to protect the trees as they grew. You see, the amount of land that is sheltered by a feature is greater by quite a factor than just the height. The trees provide far more shelter than the walls. And the sheep need shelter to survive, yet destroy the shelter that would keep them alive.'

I showed him my very sketchy sketch of the hill with curved walls. He knew exactly where I was talking about. 'Chelmorton,' he said with great delight. 'Only place like it round here. Now, when you have walls around large fields that are all straight, they are the result of the enclosures.' The enclosures were not just about hedges. Up here there would have been rich landowners wanting to extend their reach, and they would have had to use whatever they could to assert their rights (and wrongs) over the poor. 'Those fields, they are old. And the curves, well, these are done in the "Reverse-S System". When there was a team of eight oxen pulling a plough they needed to be able to turn. The curves in the walls provided the space.'

For the next five hours I was to be the driver and the student as I followed Trevor's directions and was taken on a tour of the subtle world of heavy rock. As we headed back out of Hartington I remembered my final question, just as we reached what had provoked it: that small arc of apparently retaining wall. 'I haven't a clue,' he said. 'It is very old, I see it most days, but no idea what it was built for.'

Our first stop, Trevor promised, would be very relevant to

the connections I was making between linear features and fragmentation. We were going to see a 'hedgehog smoot'.

We were passing fields separated from fields and roads by stone walls. Many walls were almost a by-product of the need to clear the fields of stones – stones left by the glaciers that began their retreat 11,000 years ago. And some of them were really rather big. For example, the glacial erratics that slid from moorland onto the peninsula of Land's End were so large they couldn't be easily removed when Iron Age farmers moved in, so they became the features of dot-to-dot field boundaries, with the gaps between filled in with smaller rocks and vegetation. These Cornish hedge banks, Oliver Rackham points out, now rank 'among the world's oldest artefacts still in use'.[3]

'There are over 5,000 miles of walls in the Peak District alone,' Trevor said. 'But with this sort of scale, can you imagine the numbers of people required to build and maintain them? There were certainly not enough people here, so as mining drew in a new population, workers came from all over the country, and with them came different visions for stone walls, different styles. There is one field in Stanton where there are five different styles in its border.' The National Stone Centre in Wirksworth has a display of nineteen different styles captured in 6-metre lengths. Georg Muller records that in Europe in 1880 there were over 5 million kilometres of walls; nowadays it's down to 2.7 million kilometres. In the UK, the figures are 270,000, down to 115,000. As for Britain's walls, Trevor made a bold claim I was not in a position to test. 'Drop me out of an aeroplane, anywhere in the country,' he said, 'and I will be able to tell you where I have landed. I know all the styles of wall. This is why I was able to win the British Championships in 1996. I studied the walls from Scotland, Wales and England.

'So, have you guessed what a smoot is yet? I'll give you a clue. There are badger smoots, sheep smoots, rabbit smoots. I made a hedgehog smoot only last week, and I didn't even know you were coming.'

We were passing a gate, which gave me just enough of a prod. Were they gates for animals?

'Not quite,' he replied, a little disappointed in me, I felt. 'Holes. They are species-specific holes in the walls.' This didn't help me much. What was the point of inserting holes into the walls that are designed to keep animals at bay?

'Take the badger smoot,' he said. 'Now, they are clever animals, and if you build a wall across a badger's path it will either undermine it or just knock it down. So we build a path for the badger. It is possible to accommodate wildlife if you are willing to shift your perspective a little and think about ways in which you can both live in some sort of harmony.'

There was a little less harmony for the rabbits, though. 'Lots of lanes, farms and people up here are all called Warren for a reason,' Trevor continued. 'There are loads of rabbits sometimes. So you might as well use them, and the smoots make that easier.' The rabbits are left in peace, and learn to use the smoots as bolt-holes, until one day the holes acquire a net on the far side, and a scare is put in the field – causing the fleeing rabbits to be easily bagged up. For some the payment for building the walls was this access to food. Another way of doing this was to have a walled area in the middle of the field, smooted, of course, and a pit within.

Sheep – well, the whole point of building these walls was to maintain discrete sheep fields, so it would seem foolish to start letting them wander. But of course Trevor had an explanation. In the corner of many of these fields there were sheepfolds, into which the flock could be rounded up for management, and these were designed to allow the sheep to be released one at a time through a 'cripple gap' or 'lunkie' – or as we now know them, a sheep smoot.

I pulled us into the drive of a small, well-kept farmhouse on the outskirts of Monyash. Trevor got out and we were greeted by a barking dog and then the firm handshake of the owner, Phil Bates. The newly landscaped garden, complete with sunken trampoline, was covered in a three-day stubble of grass. But what immediately caught my eye was the immaculate wall. A good bit of dry-stone walling looks as immovable as the most mortared construction. This was new, and, as with all these walls, deeply ancient; instantly organic, at one with its surroundings, since it is made out of its surroundings. And down at my feet, a gap. About 15 centimetres square, it was a neat space that looked as if it had always been there. The reason for taking this extra trouble was simple: the owner of the farm had come out and found a hedgehog in the garden, and did not want to build a wall that would stop it visiting. This was our hedgehog smoot.

Looking to the fields beyond the garden, though, it was clear that some of this love and attention could have been lavished on their walls. Most were more ornamental than functional. Function was provided by the wire fencing strung between posts. I suppose the amount of effort required to remove the decaying walls was so much greater than simply erecting a fence. And the land lost beneath the tumbled stones would not trouble the bottom line, as it would have been supported by subsidy.

There was no time to interrogate the landscape any further, however: Trevor had other places for me to see. As we drove off he confirmed a little more of what I already knew. The first walls up here were definitely the result of field-clearing. Some fields seem to breed stones more effectively than anything else. Glaciers retreated, dropping the burden of stone scoured from the land. In the wake of the ice came life; by 6000 BC there were red and roe deer, wild cattle and boar, pursued by Mesolithic hunter-gatherers.

Around 4000 BC Britain began the transition to agriculture, and by the late Neolithic period people had started forest clearance in what is now Derbyshire. The first records of walls date from around 2500 BC. 'They were doing it for the same reason we do, separating "horn from corn",' Trevor said. 'There is a strip of land to the east of Gardom's Edge, near Baslow, with a 500-metre-long curved stone rampart – boulders are piled 5 metres wide and 1.5 metre high – and it was defensive, probably. People lived there from 2000 BC until 1200 BC, and there were as many living there as there are now.'

As on Dartmoor, the arrival of people caused a dramatic change to the landscape. Much of the now often bleak peaks had once been covered in trees. As with other uplands, the removal of trees started in the late Neolithic, until by the eleventh century a landscape not dissimilar to today's was left. Analysis of pollen has provided some of this evidence, but there are other clues by the sides of the roads. The road signs welcoming you to villages can reveal so much. Place-names that incorporate -clough, -den, -hey, -hirst and -ley all hint at woodland, and all hark from a time before the advance of the Saxons, who left very few tree-linked names.[4]

As we got closer to the centre of Monyash Trevor pointed out a collection of surrounding fields, smaller and fairly higgledy-piggledy. These were 'runrigs': small, allotment-plot-sized fields associated with dwellings in a village and intensively cropped for vegetables. A similar system is found up in Scotland.

We stopped by a church, where Trevor wanted to explain to me the concept of 'through-stones' – stones not present in every wall, whose job is to knit the structure together. As their name suggests, they run right through the wall, sometimes sticking out on one side, giving the impression of irregular steps. Of course, they do not stick out onto the path side of the wall.

But Trevor was already eager to show me something else. The road descended a few hundred feet, and we seemed to have found ourselves in a warmer microclimate – there were more hedges around us. Trevor pointed out a mature holly tree. 'That is not a random holly,' he told me. 'Holly is, of course, evergreen. And will be planted at the point in a field where the land drains – the point at which the water flows in and out. Now, if in the winter the field floods, it will often be because the drain is blocked. And if you have planted a holly you will immediately be able to find the drain and clear it.'

As we drove on we passed through different geological zones – from sandstone to gritstone to limestone. Gritstone is like a rough sandstone, whereas limestone is harder, fossilised. Each has its own assemblage of preferred moss and lichens. 'Over sixty species of spiders have been found living in walls,' Trevor said. 'The structure lures in life – walls are a sort of linear nature reserve.'

That walls can act as a reservoir for these marvellous creatures should give them considerable additional value in the eyes of the landowner in any argument over the value of a linescape. Spiders are brilliant predators and valuable pest controllers. It has been shown that they are often the first predators to enter a field following ploughing, and can often become established before pest species have any chance of colonising it: per square metre there can be up to a thousand spiders of many different species. An interesting side-effect of the way in which many spiders hunt is that their use of webs means many more insects get caught than are eaten, making them doubly effective at controlling pests.[5]

So walls can certainly be a home to wildlife. They also, Trevor continued, enable wildlife to cross what might be considered quite a barren landscape. 'How does a stoat move, concealed, from one upland valley to the next?' he asked. 'They weave a path along and through these walls. Where can birds build a defensible nest in this frequently tree-free space? Where do the seeds of plants like the fairy foxglove shelter until the conditions spur them to germinate?

'The difference between our walls and those held together with mortar,' he continued, 'is the spaces. However well made a wall is, there will always be gaps. Just imagine life inside a simple wall – built with two lines of stones placed carefully on top of each other, leaning towards each other, and with the space in between filled with stones of varying sizes, and not forgetting the through-stones. There will be spaces, and these spaces will be used.'

'It's not just spiders, of course: woodlice, springtails, millipedes, slugs, snails, bees and wasps all make it home. These can live in the smallest of nooks. Slightly larger animals need bigger crannies. Slow worms and voles, shrews and field mice – and toads. I have found such unlikely toads in the walls – deep inside, and they look far too big to have got into the space. Hedgehogs, of course, will use larger spaces still, and use the leaf litter that will always collect around the base. More than once I have found a clutch of wheatear's pale-blue eggs. And bats, if there are small horizontal slits, will roost.' Robins and redstarts will also nest in walls, and even little owls. And the upright stones that top off a wall, 'cope-stones', are used as perches. With much of this potential habitat consisting of the interstitial spaces, is this not a good argument for allowing walls to become dilapidated?

'While some wildlife might find semi-dereliction attractive,' said Trevor, 'that is not a state we strive for. That is just one short-lived phase in the life of a wall, and once they have crumbled to less than half their height the value as a wildlife habitat is massively reduced. And you have to consider the aesthetics and functionality too.'

Of course, there is more to the non-animal life in a wall than just moss and lichens. Even the mortared walls near where I live surprise me with their life-sustaining qualities. An embellishing patch of ivy-leaved toadflax, for example: not just a pretty flower, like a mini-snapdragon, and a lovely name, but also a fascinating plant. Like most plants it is phototropic: it grows towards the light. But at the point of fertilisation it begins to grow in the opposite direction, pushing seeds into the crevices of the wall.

Down another winding road we went, through the village of Birchover, and I was instructed to pull over. Trevor got out of the car. 'Here is something I had to show you.' Even to my ignorant eye, there was something special about this wall. The top line of vertical stones was cushioned in velvet moss. The wall worked its way up the incline, yet the courses of stone, the lines in which the stones were laid, were perfectly straight. It almost looked too good to be a dry-stone wall. Then I noticed the sign:

The Mires Wall was rebuilt for the village in 2004 by: George Elliott, Craig Elliott, Trevor Wragg.

Trevor was grinning – not smug, just very proud. In front of the wall was the 'Mires Trough', mortared. 'This used to be the water supply for the whole village,' he said. 'The spring rises just behind the wall.' The water was sharply cold, clear and delicious. I was fascinated by the amazing lines he had managed to create in the Mires Wall. 'You know, I think it would have felt very different if we had used technology like spirit levels. But I was taught from the start that this is an art as well as a craft, and we are to make it "pleasing to the eye".' Which this most certainly was. I recommend a visit to this mossy, lichen-covered, organically formed wall. Near its foot, pellitory-of-the-wall, also known as lichwort, relishes the damp shade, throwing up lush leaves, towering over the cushiony yellow lichens and green liverworts.

We drove on through some of the Chatsworth estate. Once again, at a lower altitude there were more hedges, and then it was back among walls as we circled round and started to head west back to Hartington. In some places there were both hedges and walls together: hedges planted on top of walls, hedges growing alongside walls. Sometimes I imagine the plants have just taken advantage of the shelter the walls provide.

There was one last place Trevor wanted me to see. He teaches walling, which is not something very easy to teach within the confines of a classroom. You need walls. Over twenty-five years ago he searched the Peaks for a farm with walls that could do with work (which did not narrow the field down too much – I have read that up to 90 per cent of the walls up in the Peak District are in need of repair). The farm he found was just south of the village of Birchover. It is a great deal for all parties: the owner of the land, Mary Cuthbert, gets her walls rebuilt; Trevor has the perfect class-room; and the students get real hands-on experience. He took me to the edge of a field and pointed out the walls: three and a half of the four sides of the field had been completed by over 500 people. 'There is gold in them there walls,' he said. This time he was not being cryptic, however: he was being alarmingly literal.

'There was always talk of the "money-safe-stones" when I started out walling,' he explained. A money-safe-stone was one that has had a hollow worked into its upper surface in such a way that the stone can be placed in a wall and from the front look like any other. Another, usually thinner, stone is placed on top of it, but it is a subtly looser fit than the surrounding stones, which are built up as usual. The result is that, as long as you know which one is the right stone, you can slip out the guard stone, reach in, and deposit or withdraw from the hollow.

'And there was a story that came with this land,' Trevor went on. 'Many, many years ago two brothers had a farm up here on an old leadminers' pathway. One of them looked after all the money, nothing unusual about that. But then he died suddenly without telling the other brother where the money-safe-stone was. That man was driven half mad searching for it and died in poverty. Now, when I was working on this wall here,' he said, pointing to one near the trainees' field, 'I met the great-great-great-grandchildren of that farmer, and they asked me whether I had found anything interesting – the story was true, it turns out.' A few years later Trevor did indeed find the stone, but it was empty. Someone else had got there first. Now I find I cannot look at a dry-stone wall without seeking the tell-tale clues. The original stone is still there. Trevor took me to the wall and asked if I could spot it. Eventually I gave up, but as soon as his hand moved towards the answer it was so obvious. The thousands of miles of walls could contain thousands of 'safes'. I have not found another one. Yet.

Trevor showed me some of the other objects found while repairing walls. The first was a lead bell – small and dull. They had been intrigued as to where it was from, and research had revealed it to be a matins bell. I had always thought that the matins bell was one rung to call worshippers to the morning service, but this was so small it would only have stirred a lightly snoozing church mouse. Apparently it would have been struck by those entering the church.

The other find was harder to identify: two pieces of worked metal, lead again, that, when put together, formed the shape of a thin flask. It was too small to hold a drink – and in any case was in two pieces. The clue, Trevor said, was in the engraving, still just visible. There was a wall, a human figure, and a bird. This was a gunpowder case – it would have originally been held together as one with a leather tie – and was found in a wall. Perhaps a hunter had left it on a wall and it had fallen inside?

Trevor needed to get back home. I felt bloated with information and ideas. Yet even on the return journey there was more to learn, such as which field a wall belongs to. A wall, separating two fields, will reach a T-junction. Look at the join: the wall should continue in an 'L' to one side, but start again on the other. This shows which farmer has responsibility for it. As I parked up in Hartington I noticed that Trevor's road was called Stonewell Lane. Not quite nominative determinism, but not far off.

It was sad to say goodbye to Trevor; my admiration for his dedication and knowledge had already become fondness. As we parted he handed me a piece of stone he had picked up along the way; he thought I should not leave without a collection of 'Derbyshire screws'. 'You work it out,' he said as I got back into the car to begin the long journey home.

The chunk of limestone was covered in fossilised something, but I had no idea what. It had to wait until I was back in the world of the internet. At the first motorway services I pulled in, too impatient to wait till I was back to Oxford, and searched online. Crinoids! Marine animals distantly related to the starfish and other echinoderms. While there are still around 600 species nowadays, they used to be one of the most abundant life forms in Palaeozoic oceans. And now, forming the stones that help this linescape to thrive, they create habitat for other wildlife.

*

Soon after my trip around the Peaks I had another opportunity to meander across Dartmoor. Every time I visit I feel as though I shed a little weight from my shoulders. This time I decided to take a closer look at its walls – there are hedges on Dartmoor but, just as in the Peaks, they tend to be concentrated at lower altitude.

Up on the moor the air was lung-scouringly fresh, and the visibility minimal, but the walls had come to resemble miniature rainforests, so richly embroidered were they with lichen, liverwort and moss. You could even find pockets of real rainforest: trees dripping epiphytes, gauzy pale beards – treebeard. Clearly there is an issue of scale, and we are not talking massive dangling lianas, but shift your perspective and you will find great beauty.

I had always been a bit dismissive of the sedums – the large genus of small succulent plants that makes its home in the most inhospitable, soil-free crevices. A while back I was taken to the top of Canary Wharf, for a feature I was writing about living roofs, to see the planting done up there, which included a bed of sedum: not a thrilling sight. But here, on Dartmoor stones, framed by lichen and moss, I found a sedum called English stonecrop, with dangling pale flowers on red stems. Not massive and spectacular: just pretty and perfect.

Of the wall-living and -loving plants the most common, after the mosses, are the ferns, and the most distinctive, to my mammal-centric world-view, is the hart's tongue fern. Now I looked closely to try and see how these single-fronded plants were able to hold on to the rock. It was almost as if at one point there was a place where plant and stone were one. There is magic in the closeness of plant and rock: sometimes they can conflict, and the plants will undermine the stones, but here it was lichen-like symbiosis, but this time between animate and inanimate. Slightly above one hart's tongue, and next to a profusion of common polypody, was green spleenwort. All of these wall- and rock-loving plants tend to favour the wetter west of the country, but the advent of the railway network provided both a sheltered, damp habitat and a means for dispersal all over the country.

There must be something about the feel of a place that

comes from its deep history, from how it was formed? The Peak District is made of sedimentary rock, layers of sand compressed for 400 million years. Dartmoor is set amid sedimentary rock, but is itself Britain's largest lump of granite. Not long (geologically at least) after the stone of the Peaks was laid, a pluton – a rather pleasing word for 'body of igneous rock' – crystallised from slowly cooling magma just below the surface of what is now Devon. The action of weathering since the Carboniferous period resulted in the emergence of this myth-ridden moor. Over 160 tors, granite outcrops, on the moor are flags to the bedrock. And up here smoots become 'creeps'. Superficially these spaces can feel similar, but there is something strangely ancient about Dartmoor, despite its rocks being of similar age to the Peak District's. It feels as though they have seen more life.

Stones seem such an unlikely foundation for much life, but the walls of Britain have created a network that, while not rivalling the hedge for diversity, contributes so much to the ability of wildlife to move through the landscape, connecting and spreading. Sometimes very slowly, as lichens inch to the corners of the compass. Sometimes with the sneaky speed of a stoat on a mission.

5

Ancient Paths and Green Lanes

We have all walked along ancient tracks and green lanes. The concrete path that runs from my home to the primary school was once a green lane. The busy road that runs parallel to it was a path that cut through farmland. These lines have been walked into the landscape. They were the routes that took the post-glacial hunter-gatherers across the land; that linked the earliest settlements and evolved, in many cases, into the roads we have today. Those that have survived the onslaught of progress present us with a connection – connecting us to the wildlife that thrives in the tunnels of green or along the ridges, and also connecting us to the history of the people whose feet created these paths. It is impossible to walk these ways without feeling something more: an echo of previous lives. It is not hard to find a way into this history. There are still ancient paths to be followed when you know the names – the Harroway, from Dover to Cornwall, or the Icknield Way from the Dorset coast to Norfolk, for example. The path with which I am most familiar is the Ridgeway, the section of the Icknield Way that runs for 140 kilometres from Ivinghoe Beacon in east Buckinghamshire to West Kennet in Wiltshire. And whenever the opportunity arises I gather family and friends to explore one particular segment.

Twenty miles to the west of Oxford you come to Uffington. Parking below the escarpment on a recent August outing, we looked up, as always, in wonder at the white horse carved into the hill, just beneath the Ridgeway. Our small gang headed on towards our mission, which was to join in with the bank-holiday re-whitening.

For something like this to have remained as such a startling beacon since the late Bronze Age (it is possibly 3,000 years old), there needs to be some maintenance. And with the White Horse over 100 metres long, this needs to be a deed of the community, not just an individual. So it is not surprising to find that there used to be a custom called 'scouring', which would take place every seven years. But when that became irregular the National Trust stepped in, and now Spring and August Bank Holiday weekends are when we can all make a difference. The work is perfect for those suffering from stress, as it requires you to sit with a bucket of lumps of chalk and a hammer, mashing the chalk into the outline of the horse.

As ancient as the horse is, compared to the path it remains a mere foal. There is evidence of people using this route for the last 5,000 years, and it is hard to imagine that Neolithic settlers did not use it earlier than that. It is the sensible track to take: the ridges gave an easier passage than the damp or forested lowlands. There is a compromise in taking the high road, though: finding water high up on porous chalk land is always going to be a struggle.

After we had had our fill of smashing chalk we ambled up to the top to look down over the horse and the plain before us. The ability to envision the shape of a horse that would be visible from the air (easily the best place from which to view the horse as a horse) while pretty much invisible to anyone standing on it, I find delightfully baffling.

We gave the hill fort above us just a cursory glance because we had another goal in mind. We were heading towards the magical monument of Wayland's Smithy. The path was white and the sun just hazy enough behind gently moving clouds for it to be a perfect day for walking. Soon the gaggle of four adults and six children was spread out over quite a distance. Those lagging were doing so for the very best of reasons. There is plenty to distract on a path so old.

Wayland's Smithy is just off the main route of the Ridgeway and has been dated even earlier than the path itself, which would argue that the path was in existence well before dateable artefacts were identified. In fact the Smithy is a Neolithic long barrow, dating from 3590 BC. That is a thousand years before the Ancient Egyptians were building pyramids. And while it might not have the drama of Giza, the Smithy has a charm all of its own. The name comes with its own mythology, but was attached to the barrow 4,000 years after its construction when Saxons found the tomb. Wayland was a god of the smithy, and the story goes that if your horse throws a shoe you can leave it, with a silver coin, at the Smithy, and in the morning it will be shod. Over 50 metres long and 10 metres wide, the grass-covered barrow covering the tomb is now surrounded by majestic beech trees, creating a theatre of calm, ideal for the imagining of such tales. The adults sat down to a welcome Thermos flask, the children made merry, sustained occasionally by cake, leaping across the entrance stones to the amazing mound.

We did not have a horse in need of help, but offerings could be made to a woman sitting calmly to one side of the monument, in such harmony with her surroundings that she might have been there for centuries. On the blanket of organic colours spread out in front of her were pendants, beautiful stones. The children were transfixed, a lot of pocket money was spent, and on the return journey many stories were created as these new ancient talismans spun webs of wonder, not least about magical places that had already vanished like Atlantis beneath the surrounding sea of agriculture.

Until very recently the Ridgeway passed through some of Britain's most diverse flora. Unploughed chalk grassland is a habitat rich in flowers, but these days, thanks to massive improvements in agriculture, short on acres. In the last sixty years over 80 per cent of it has gone, and when you think that just a square metre of chalk grassland can contain forty different plant species you realise just how special it can be. Thanks to its diversity of plants the area around the White Horse is a Site of Special Scientific Interest (SSSI). Species include dwarf thistle, bird's-foot trefoil, wild thyme, horseshoe vetch, yellow wort and the rare Chiltern gentian. It is not an easy habitat in which to flourish, but plants have evolved to cope with the pressures of grazing by growing leaves and buds close to the soil surface, though of course the flowers must raise their heads if they are to get the attention they crave from pollinators.

A line like the Ridgeway has the potential to help protect what remains. Scheduled Ancient Monuments, such as the Smithy, have legal protection that can help the surrounding ecosystems by constraining the activities that can take place there. The margin that is held as a sanctuary will differ for different monuments, but the greater the amount that can be scheduled, the greater the restraint on plough and spray.

Despite the great potential of this land, the most obvious plants we saw that day were dandelions and nettles taking advantage of the richer soil beside the path. Patches of old thorn hedge created sheltered corridors, but then they would peter out into little more than a ditch, while the prairie-like farmland stretched away silent but for the occasional skylark, and rooks making use of the ash and hazel clumps.

One reason for so much potential diversity is a soil so thin that it is little more than a few coats of brown paint on the white chalk canvas. As we walked I tried to get the children to understand how this chalk tells stories as fantastical as anything their faery minds could come up with. How we were walking across the bottom of a subtropical ocean; how in the Upper Cretaceous period, around 100 million years ago, the seabed, littered with the remains of micro-organisms, countless calcite coccoliths, was rucked up by the same geological processes that lifted the Alps. Once again, the value is in the very impoverishment. If the sward is slathered in fertiliser it become far more productive, but at the cost of its ability to support diversity.

The trees were fully fledged in summer leaf. In the beech hangers the treetops shaped themselves together into an enticing bun. The name 'hangers' comes from branches that hang out over the land as the trees claim the slopes for their own. When the winter winds have stripped them bare these hummocks of trees adorning the tops of hills to the north of the Ridgeway are known by some as 'hedgehogs'.

The Ridgeway has lasted so long because the main routes nowadays from A to B have been cut with engines and ingenuity to keep journeys short, while the Ridgeway is not the short route any more. It is the path to take to think, and sink into the history, both human and natural, that created the route – history that has been erased from much of the rest of the island. There are other ancient paths, but they tend to be less well defined; cryptic trails that need a little research. The ones I love most are known as green lanes.

Green lanes are defined as different things by different people, but their essence is clear: they are lanes that have been walked into the land. They are unmetalled, and usually bounded by hedges, walls or ditches. They are not necessarily rights of way, but they were once the highways of the land. Some ride the ridges, others sink into softer ground.

Remember the history of those feet. First following animal trails, perhaps, at a time when such tracks were more wild than peopled; then linking farms, facilitating early trade. Then animals began to be used to carry the burdens of our lives, and then gradually the tracks were widened to accommodate inventions like the sledge – less efficient than wheels, but cheaper and easier to make. The friction of the runners would have gouged the tracks down deeper into the land, creating ruts like those left by wheels, that in turn formed runnels down which water would flow, further scoring the route into the planet. We have always changed the land, and our lines are some of the clearest evidence.

My first conscious encounter with a green lane came in 1993, while radio-tracking hedgehogs in Devon. Walking back to my caravan-home as dawn crept over the hill, I spotted a herd of roe deer. We watched each other for a while before they turned and almost immediately vanished from sight. Intrigued, I crossed the field and found a gap in the hedge that opened out into a tunnel of green. Slightly sunken, with hedges on either side long since grown out into treelines, here was an old path over this hill. I walked along it for around a hundred metres until a more substantial hedge blocked the way. Within this hidden world there was a real sense of peace – though it was far from unsullied by modern life. People working on the farm had been taking advantage of its invisibility to get rid of fertiliser bags and other rubbish. Back at the caravan I studied the Ordnance Survey map. There was no hint of a path where I had been: just a field margin. And this made me wonder how many other secret lines there were around the country. Who better to talk to than Valerie Belsey, the author of a book called *The Green Lanes of England*?

Valerie was waiting for me in Staverton at the bus stop by the pub that would have once been a drovers' rest. She has a robust elegance that comes from years mixing her love of the outdoors with another life as a musician. She guided me off these narrow Devon lanes onto even narrower ones, my car brushing the banked hedges with both wing mirrors, until I was silently begging the world to keep oncoming traffic at bay.

'The majority of roads and paths in this country are, or rather were, green lanes,' she told me. 'Not all are sunken holloways. They were the equivalent of the roads, railways and internet of now. Between the Romans and the turnpikes, pretty much every route was a green lane. In fact, there was no centralised road-building in this country until 1919 and the arrival of national town planning.'

As we emerged out of the lanes onto a hill the steep hedges dropped away, taking with them their claustrophobic atmosphere. The view across the rolling patchwork landscape was grand enough to make me pull over and stop. In the far distance was Hay Tor – one of the most accessible of the granite growths that spatter Dartmoor. Above our heads, as we got out and breathed the summer morning air more deeply, was the beautiful musical dance of another skylark. I notice the skylark for more than its musical majesty. I notice it because it is there. It has survived, albeit in diminished numbers, the industrialisation of our land.

Getting her bearings, Valerie pointed down into the valley. This land belonged to Riverford's, one of Britain's largest organic vegetable-box delivery companies. And at our feet was a field of lucerne. This pea-like plant is part of Riverford's green manure regime. It is a bit of a wonder-plant, absorbing nitrogen from the air and pulling up nutrients from deeper soils. Why bother spraying with expensive fertilisers when there are plants that can do the work for you?

Valerie was pointing at the patchwork. 'You can make out some of the lanes from up here,' she said, sketching them with her finger. 'Those bigger lines are all leading towards the moor.' A hundred years ago this area had been smothered in flax to supply material for the war effort. Again, here was a snapshot of the land that felt permanent – yet was steeped in many histories. I was excited by the juxtaposition of fields of varying greens and browns, with the almost uniformly dark-green lines. The rich green of summer had been allowed to mature in the hedges and lane. Only the pylons, looping their loads and striding at odds with the hedges and lanes below, added a certain dissonance.

Later, over tea in her Totnes cottage, Valerie would show me on a map how these green paths ran down from the high ground like streams. 'This is because they were drovers' routes, running to temporary summer pastures in the moor's shadow, allowing the winter pastures to recover and also be harvested for the harsher weather.' Staverton was a key point on the drovers' routes, from where in the summer they had taken cattle up onto the fringes of Dartmoor, to give the fields of the South Hams time to recover for the winter. Transhumance was the name for this practice of moving livestock and all or part of a community from one area of grazing to another. 'So busy were these lanes that I often wonder what the interactions would be like – there are often no obvious passing-places, and two herds or flocks coming head-to-head was probably a fraught business.'

Back on our way, we followed the undulations deeper into the closest we get to Tolkien's Shire this side of Middle Earth.

An old, unused gateway, just beside a rather surprising tower of ivy, offered a parking space. On closer inspection, I saw that supporting this tall cylinder of green was not a massive tree, but a slate chimney, some 20 metres tall, and I was rather taken aback by such an industrial intrusion into this otherwise bucolic idyll of tall trees and tiny lanes. 'You forget that this is a post-industrial landscape,' said Valerie. 'This land was teeming with people; just over that wall there is a vertical drop, the face of the quarry that this chimney was a part of. The slate from here went all over the country. I will try and find you some – it is an amazing blue.'

We walked down the small road for a short while, and then had to shrink into the ferny wall. A tractor, swiftly followed by a quad bike, came careering around the corner. So little changes. Then the way was blocked. The tractor, complete with trailer, had turned sideways, forcing us to clamber onto the bank to get around. And there was the quad-bike, two men and a dog. I noticed we were at a junction of five lanes, and it quickly became apparent that there were not enough of them to bar all options to whatever was expected to emerge from the green lane (down which we were due to head). So Valerie and I were swiftly recruited to block one lane just as the first sounds of the incoming herd were heard. Bullocks, loads of them, streaming up towards us, goaded on by another quad-bike. The timing was perfect. Here were the lanes still being used for one of their original purposes. Valerie was clearly delighted.

The bustle of work moved on, and as we headed downhill soon, apart from the spare pips and cheeps of mid-morning birds, the sound of our feet and the occasional murmur of wind, we were in a silent world. Banks rose as we sank down. In places the reason for the sinking path was clear, the bare stone testifying to the occasional watercourse it had become.

These were the highways of an earlier age, quiet now because most industry had long since slipped away. People had used these paths to move livestock, as they still do, but also to get to work. The mine owners did not build houses for their workers: they had to walk in to work, and these were the only paths. In fact, there is evidence that when the weather was not too bad many of them would use the lanes as temporary dormitories.

When noise stops, the silence that ensues can be all the more intense, and so it was as I slipped into imagining this spot back in the time of my distant ancestors. Not, again, that there really was quite silence. The stream that deepened the path was trickling with the previous day's rain; there was a buzz in the hedge banks, and a willow warbler garnished a goat willow with song.

Wildlife can flourish in these lanes: the quiet, the shelter, and the depth of history all lead to potentially great diversity. And of course it is no surprise that they would be a haven: their defining feature is their boundaries – hedges and walls. These are lines rich in life, life that would and does supplement the diets of those passing through. In his poem 'The Lane', Edward Thomas, writing about the lanes of Essex, conjures this fecundity:

Some day, I think, there will be people enough
In Froxfield to pick all the blackberries

Out of the hedges of Green Lane, the straight
Broad lane where now September hides herself
In bracken and blackberry, harebell and dwarf gorse.[1]

Our early July walk was guided by the square stems and
purple flowers of salad burnet, the powder puffs of meadowsweet, bitter cress, yellow vetch and enough horseflies to
keep us from dawdling, though in earlier times people would
have dawdled, harvesting as they went. Salad burnet's young-
est leaves taste a little like cucumber; meadowsweet is, as the
name suggests, sweet and can be eaten, or used to scent a
room. Just around the bend was lady's bedstraw – another
name that holds the key to previous uses, in this case for
stuffing mattresses, as it has a reputation as both an insect
repellent and a sedative. Cresting a large hedge-bound holly
was a magisterial toupee of honeysuckle. Applying Hooper's
Rule to this lane we found its hedge to be around 600 years
old, and since the path is defined by its hedges, we can argue
that the path was at least 600 years old as well.

But the ecological value of a green lane can even exceed
that of a hedge. There is a 'green-lane effect', whereby the
inside faces of the hedges that bound the lane tend to be
warmer, more sheltered and more attractive to wildlife than
the outside faces, creating a microclimatic tunnel within
which wildlife, should the surrounding fields be forgiving,
can flourish. As we have already seen, finding over 2,000
individual species in an 85-metre stretch is not unreasonable.

These paths are historical monuments to a life lived less
hurriedly – to the pace of our feet, or the gait of a horse.

Such aspects of the past I do crave. And I yearn for the sheer volume of biomass there would have been. We live in such denuded times – it was only later I realised that the delight I had felt that day at the sight of a dragonfly coursing the path was a symptom. Golden-ringed dragonflies are beautiful. But just the one majestic predator during our entire walk? Yes, big, fierce animals have to be rare; their numbers often controlled by the small, less fierce animals on which they feed. But we are faced with a world lacking the amount of life necessary to reach its potential, and that makes me sad.

Cleverly Valerie managed, over our four hours of rambling, to wind us round along a series of green lanes in a sort of circle. Despite there being over 800 kilometres of green lane in South Devon, she has an instinctive reading of the land that acts like an inbuilt sat nav. As we neared the car she stooped and picked up a piece of stone to hand to me. 'I promised to find you some of that special slate.' Not until we were out of the overhanging trees was there enough light to examine the thin stone more carefully. Of course she was right: it was dark grey with a hint of blue. And it was a reminder that this had been a heavily worked landscape, the lines within it having changed beyond the imaginings of the workers who trod them down.

After a cup of tea I left Valerie for my return home, along busy roads that were once, I am sure, green lanes in their own right. The constant is change.

*

The biggest threat these lanes face is neglect – left alone for long enough they will become absorbed into the fabric of the land. The next biggest threat they face is being discovered.

The trouble with green lanes is their definition. Legally, 'green lane' means nothing. It is merely descriptive and symbolic. It tends to denote routes that are not tarmacked and are bounded on at least one side by a hedge. Valerie proposed a more encompassing name – Green Routes Used Throughout History, or GRUTHs.

There is a 'definitive map' of public rights of way in England and Wales, on which green lanes appear nowhere. Restricted byways, such as footpaths and bridleways, are well known – and they may also be green lanes. There are also 'byways open to all traffic', known as BOATs, which differ from unclassified roads in normally being used only by people on foot or horseback. They too might be green lanes. And these are where the trouble can begin. BOATs are out there waiting for conquest by the brave adventurers in their 4 x 4s.

Welcome to the world of GLASS, the Green Lane Association. They describe themselves as a group 'for those who enjoy using the Country's network of ancient unsurfaced public roads and vehicular rights of way'. And they paint a picture of respect for the land that they seek to conquer.

I wrote to the chairman of GLASS, Duncan Green, to find out more about their campaign to keep these lanes open to motorised vehicles. In addressing the potential conflict between motorists and ramblers, the response was quite revealing. 'We both have those with extreme views,' said Mr Green. 'Drivers who do not follow our codes and give way, walkers who insist on following the exact legal line, and causing upland erosion due to large numbers.' Well, yes, an excess of walkers can cause considerable erosion, but to condemn as 'extreme' those who walk along paths designed for feet is a little rich. On the other hand, it is hard to imagine anything more likely to disturb the qualities of a green lane, one that has been worn into place by the feet of thousands of people, than the gouging prowess of tons of metal. There have been many conflicts. I have stood my ground when confronted by such vehicles; when we have equal rights of way I am not leaping into a hedge just to benefit the machine. That is the way bullies work.

Some paths, including high-profile routes like the Ridgeway, have been seriously threatened by off-roaders. I remember a winter walk where sections of path were so deeply rutted by bikes and cars that they had frozen into a miniature mountain range, sharp ridges of icy mud that made walking hazardous.

'Historically,' Jeff Goddard from the Friends of the Ridgeway told me, 'the main threat was its abuse by the off-road community, both 4 x 4 recreational SUVs and trail bikes, which were legal on the BOAT sections that predominated south of the Thames; however, a long campaign in which the Friends played a leading part was eventually rewarded by the award of Restricted Byway status that has made such use illegal over the greater part of the route, leading to a welcome recovery of the surface and environment. Only the southern end remains covered only by seasonal TRO (Traffic Regulation Order).'

A further problem with the appearance of these vehicles on green lanes and other ancient paths is one of pace. For thousands of years, millions of steps have been taken along these lines. Walking has made the lines. One step after another. You could not imagine Richard Long's famous 1967 photographic piece, *A Line Made by Walking*, created in any other way. The walking pace of progress has been set deep into us. For nearly two million years we have been walking. It is only in the blink of an evolutionary eye that we have sped up our lives from 3 miles per hour. We have evolved to live at that pace; we have evolved to think at that pace. The great brains that accompany us as we walk are excellent at adapting, but still, we are at our best when we slow down. Which is why the insult of exhaust and speed that imposes on a peaceful afternoon on a green lane is so intrusive.

The only way green lanes can be maintained for their historic purpose of providing a linescape for feet to follow is for feet to follow them; for them to be used. Remember, neglect is the biggest threat. So find your lanes, walk your lanes, love your lanes.

There is something intimately comforting about being surrounded by green. Green lane walking, at its best, can give me the impression of being made tiny enough to amble inside a hedgerow. It is easier to enter this world alone, I find. So one spring day, visiting my mother-in-law in Dorset and finding that everyone else was going out, I decided to treat myself to an expedition. There are many old lanes around her home not far from Lyme Regis – some now roads, though so narrow and so overgrown with vegetation as to be little different from the green lanes they once were. I headed out without a destination in mind, along sunken metalled roads that curled languidly around hills, until I came to a signpost for a footpath. Up a track past a farm, and there, as the hedge banks on either side quickly rose up, the tarmac ended.

Then came a moment, I think when the tractor tracks gave up too, when I felt I had crossed a threshold into a different version of the world. Green had grown uninterrupted across the lane, and the walls began to close in around me. The sunken lane's steep sides furred with furtive ferns – twilight plants relishing the damp shade. Where the sun broke through, foxgloves leapt up – wonderful plants; I have always loved the lewd openness of the flowers and their promiscuous seduction of bumblebees. They have names to play with: bloody bells, cow flop, dog's lugs, fairy gloves, lustmore, pop dock, throat root and witches' thimbles. Part of the cocktail of drugs that kept my mother going through her illness was the digoxin derived from this prodigious plant. All too soon a wall of bramble and nettle blocked my path. I felt there must be more, so I headed up to my right, and found a remarkable field. A sloping duvet of a field, rich in saturation with buttercups and studded with clover.

The spring sun, I noticed, had now vanished, and that noise I had originally presumed to be a military jet was in fact coming from one of the more pillared clouds. I was nearly an hour from the cottage, so reasoned that as long as I could get back into the lane I would find some shelter.

All I could see was a dense line of trees making a pretty impenetrable barrier. I followed it around the hillside looking for a gap. Something had vanished: the drone of the A35 that had been tethering me to the real world had gone – perhaps with the oncoming storm the wind had shifted direction. Still I could find no way back in.

In the end it was the badgers that provided the clue: a faint line laid in the grass that led me to a gap beyond the largely superfluous wire, which seemed to swallow me and then spill me down as I slipped on unexpected slickness. I stumbled back to my feet in another world again. Back under a green arch in a true holloway. It was easy to see how these paths became the refuge for recusant priests and others who had fallen foul of the authorities. Deep within the green I felt hidden and safe.

I was not a moment too soon, and while I doubt there was any judgement in the electrifying clash of elements, I was most certainly beset. Peering up through the contorted trunks of once-laid hawthorn, I could see the torrential downpour – nothing short of a natural power-shower. As always, it takes a while for the water to weave its path through the leaves, but there was no way I was going to stay dry. Within a few minutes the rain was pouring through the foliage. But the thunder had retreated into the distance and time meant I had to start the return journey, the lines to either side still hedge-ish, but mostly grown into twisted trees, hearts open to the world, knots rotted into perfect holes for wildlife to shelter.

By the time I made it to the tarmac the rain had ceased, and the sky gave no hint of the fury it had unleashed a short while before. The road told a different story. A stream of mud coursed down the lane to my right. I once commented to a friend who sells vegetables from her farm on how clean hers were. It was foolish to give away the soil that nurtures you, she pointed out to me: she makes sure she leaves as much as possible on the land where it belongs. But here I was seeing a small river of topsoil, charging around the corner and down, eventually, to the sea.

The disaster of industrial agriculture was captured in that scene. Fields left bare over winter, soil compacted as subsidised maize for the biofuel market is managed with heavy machinery. Fertility dwindles, and is remedied with compound fertilisers that require such massive injections of energy that if the cradle-to-grave analysis was done on this industrial planting we would see the true lunacy.

The next day, dried out but still buzzing from the deep-lane experience and the walk of a holloway, I decided to try and lure the rest of the family into that hidden world.

From the kitchen sink in my mother-in-law's cottage there is a fantastic view across to Chardown. After dinner the perfect digestive is a gentle walk to the top, from where the sinking sun, if so minded, can cast the most golden hue. Only those with the knowledge would recognise the dog-guarded driveway up a very narrow lane as the portal to an almost invisible path that leads onto a beautiful green lane.

So we walked, or in the case of my boy, Pip, scampered, around the hill within a tunnel of green. The hedge on our left was old and grown out, but the trees bore the evidence of the wounding of years gone by. Disarticulated and unnaturally angular, the aged thorns were accompanied by hazel and holly. The tramping feet of time had made their mark on the hedge bank: the top of the bank, holding on to last year's hart's-tongue fern, which looked very bedraggled next to fresh lords and ladies, reached head height. The exposed roots formed a wattle-wall that in places looked like dancing figures writhing around one another, in others, where the soil had gone completely, like a window out to sea. As we broke out of the tunnel to top the hill, the air was instantly fresher. Gone was the shelter of the lane – from damp ferny walls to sheep-shorn grass in a few steps.

At the top, I always marvel at how flat this hill is. A line of gorse running across the middle is used for shelter by the sheep, its thorns capturing wool among the tropically scented flowers like monstrous thistledown. And right at the lip of the drop down to my mother-in-law's house, the tree that stood in strong evening silhouette was, I was sure as I crept closer to it, a thorn bush. But closer inspection proved it to be a sheep- and deer-mauled holly. Every single leaf within reach of the ground was gone, leaving a slightly contorted lollipop of a tree.

Looking north, out over the ever green Marshwood Vale, it was now easy to see a scene of both fragmentation and connection. The clichéd patchwork of small fields held in check by dark green lines was a landscape chopped into bite-sized pieces. Yet so many of those lines were more than just hedges: they were paths, weaving through them a rich ecosystem that allowed both wildlife and us greater freedom to move.

The edge overlooking the cottage is not as precipitous as it appears from below, so we observed the tradition of the children phoning their Nana so we could wave, our silhouettes clear in the setting sun.

6

Canals

There is, I thought, no comparison between a canal and a river. One is natural, organic, flowing and full of life, the other a concrete ditch of stagnant water populated by shopping trolleys and mattresses. One is fed from an entire catchment, fed by springs and the rain, the other reliant on the vestiges of the industrial revolution just to keep afloat. Where are you going to see an otter, an embodiment of all that is wild? A river is the natural home for an otter.

I love our patch of the Thames, the Long Bridges nature reserve, hidden away from the main drag, where we swim each summer. There used to be a formal swimming place here, with changing-rooms, diving boards and ladders. Now all that is left are the concreted banks. But the mown grass begs for picnics and the water, oh, how little there is that matches leaping in on a hot day. Actually, there is something, and that is the delight on the children's faces as they do the same, in particular my fearless 'odd-daughter' Naia. And swimming with my head up, not for fear of the water, but to be alert for the kingfishers that hunt this stretch.

Canal water, on the other hand, seems merely a septic cistern to be avoided like the plagues it carries.

Thus my prejudice remained neatly intact. I had every expectation of it being confirmed when I accepted an invitation from the then Canal Laureate, Jo Bell, to accompany her on a journey down to Stratford-upon-Avon on her barge *Tinker*. She needed help with the locks (two days and thirty-nine locks, which, for those who are not experienced with such things, is a lot), and there was the added advantage that Jo happened to have a previous incarnation as an industrial archaeologist.

The day before I was due to begin my poetic cruise the family was invited to a birthday picnic on the Cherwell, a tributary of the Thames that flows through Oxford. My wife Zoe suggested that, rather than hire a punt like everyone else, we could use the Canadian canoe in which we have a share, and paddle up to join the fun. The four of us linked up with another family and began our adventure.

Going upstream from the boathouse and towards Oxford always reminds you of the power of the river, and it was with a degree of relief that we snuck off to the right and onto the Cherwell. Immediately we were into magical *Wind in the Willows* territory – arching trees striving to complete a tunnel. And then into university territory, manicured yet beautiful. Magdalen College School and the bridge over which we have cycled innumerable times both benefit from a change of perspective. And then a choice: a fork in the river, and we followed our friends to the right.

How quickly things changed. Still a river, an organic, flowing, living thing. But the atmosphere altered, a ramping-up of something ever since we had left the boathouse. This living stream was as controlled and canalised as, well, a canal. The banks of even the main stretch of the Thames were reinforced and determined, but here on the Cherwell it was extreme. Some brutalist architecture rose up to our right, and the bed of the stream rose up to meet our hull. Our oars were now scraping the bottom, and a small reef of shopping trollies entangled with weeds created an island. An unlikely atoll; home to sci-fi claws of alien crayfish.

This was not a world without life – an ash oozed through a drain's outflow, buddleia obstinately clung to the walls, and another ash had set about systematic destruction of the brick-work, its roots ripping bricks from mortar with slow-motion ease. But there was an air of menace – I was half-expecting to find my oar caught on a corpse. Yet this was a river. And also, it transpired, the wrong arm of the river, as we reached a dead-end and had to retrace our strokes and re-join the correct stem and on to our more bucolic destination.

By the time we lifted the canoe out of the river back at the boathouse at the end of the day, I realised how aware I had become of the control that had been exerted over what had once been a wild and organic thing. This river, this watery behemoth, had been tamed – not completely, and far from perfectly, but the wild wandering days of the Thames are no more.

It is not and cannot be a canal. For the heart of the difference is in the source of the water and its flow. The river receives rain and spring and it flows; the canal is topped up by a reservoir, and the water does not flow. Or it does, as the locks draw down more water, but only sort of. That night

I slept deeply, vaguely feeling the memory of rocking in the twilight of my consciousness. By morning I was well aware of muscles that had been used.

Catching the wandering Jo Bell was not easy. She was booking in crew to accompany her all the way from Staffordshire, through Birmingham and on to Stratford-upon-Avon. Each exchange of willing slaves required some contact with the rail/road network. But where she was going to be stopping for the night was unpredictable. So I took a bike.

I got the train to Birmingham International and cycled the half-hour to Catherine de Barnes. As the road rose to the hump of a bridge, I noticed a short line of longboats to my left, and beside the penultimate one there was Jo, in her trademark cap, deep in technical conversation with her boiler-suited neighbour for the night.

Tinker is her home, and for the next two days I was to help Jo move her home to Stratford, where she was to become a bard in residence. Black with white and red trimmings, *Tinker* is a smart, if clearly lived-in, boat. Short-haired, determined and well-lived, Jo is also smart: razor-sharp smart.

While I have had many narrowboat experiences – my wife used to live on one – an induction into a new boat's idiosyncrasies is essential. These are almost organic beings, they have personalities – and certainly 'things you must not do'. An indication of *Tinker*'s character was the red blackboard on the cupboard in the kitchen, on which was written, 'If we're not supposed to dance, why all this music?' Jo's messages to herself, and all visitors, change according to wind and whim.

Visitors. I was not going to have the poet all to myself. I

would be sharing her and *Tinker* with the bestselling crime writer Helen Cadbury, a warm-hearted woman you would not expect to have quite such a fascination with the macabre. The following days would reveal how our minds were reading everything in slightly different ways. We were both looking for material for our very different books.

Essential lessons: do not try to talk to Jo while she is steering the boat from anywhere other than right beside her. Make tea and bring it to the captain at regular intervals. Locks are dangerous if you are an idiot. Don't be an idiot. In fact, by the end of the first day we were promised that we would have a case of 'Locker's Bottom'. Disappointingly this was not going to be twelve bottles of fine ale, but two cases of abused gluteus maximus muscles.

Locks are at the heart of the canal system. They are used to lift or lower boats, and there is a rhythm to it all that can be really very pleasing. We were heading downhill on the Grand Union Canal, so when we approached a lock what we wanted to find was that someone had just come uphill, leaving it full of water, saving us time and effort. Unfortunately most people appeared to be heading in the same direction as us, and both Helen and I were soon noticing interesting new muscles.

We moved at walking pace, and slower still when passing moored boats whose crockery would be disturbed by any unruly turns of speed. There is good cause to keep slow. The wake, the ripple of a wave that spreads out from the stern in a V, must not break on the bank – the energy from this wash undermines the bank, causing it to tumble into the water, taking with it vegetation that then puts down root and flourishes anew, thereby narrowing the channel. Soon such narrowing would cause the canal to become unusable and, as with the green lanes, result in their functional demise. We know this will happen, as it already has.

Parliamentary Acts for navigational improvement have been in place since 1425, when the improvements were made to the River Lea. The sixteenth century saw more substantial changes to Britain's rivers, extending their navigable reach, cutting new channels and using simple locks to regulate the flow of water, in each case driven by the inexorable spread of commerce – carrying goods by water was much cheaper and safer than across land.

The Navigations, as they are known, became more assertive in controlling the water and allowing access to larger vessels. For example, in the early eighteenth century, the Aire and Calder Navigation opened up Leeds to business, and soon a thriving trade of woollen goods was heading east and wool and corn were heading west back to Leeds.

The growth of the network was stimulated by the tremors of the Industrial Revolution, at the same time as being a catalyst for the remarkable changes about to be unleashed on Britain and the world. In 1761 Francis Egerton, the third Duke of Bridgewater, instigated the breakthrough, with his canal taking coal from his estate in Worsley to the industrial heart of Manchester. This was 'the first canal to take a course independent of rivers'.[1] The Bridgewater Canal sparked 'canal mania', as the obvious benefits of these newly laid lines became apparent. The cost of coal in the city fell by 50 per cent and investment in this new technology soared. By the 1830s the canal network extended to over 6,400 kilometres. The North Sea could be reached from Liverpool. Access by water was once determined by topography, but canals could and did cut across watersheds, through hills and over valleys, linking industry and people like never before.

The Grand Union, on which we were travelling, linked Birmingham and London: 220 kilometres and 166 locks that could be managed in a little over three days, if the horse did not need a rest. We planned to be a little less ambitious. To start with it was just horses. A single horse can manage one eighth of a ton on its own, 2 tons pulling a wagon on a hard road, but 50 tons pulling a barge on a canal. Now, all our horses fit under a bonnet.[2]

While horses were still being used on the canals well into the twentieth century, most commercial use moved on to steam and then diesel. But one thing did stay similar. The pace. Even now, with powerful engines at narrow-boaters' disposal, there is a strict 4 mph speed limit on the nation's canals.

This walking-pace world was not to last, and the canal was swiftly overtaken by rail and then road as the principal method of transport. This was more than just a passive shift; there was an active campaign on the part of the new railways to see that the canals were crushed. At the heart of this was the unrelenting determination of the free market; within twenty years of the first commercial railways, the passion for everything rail had resulted in emergent companies buying up the canals to smother competition. They introduced such high fees that most hauliers were forced out of the water and onto the rail.

Actually, the railways would not have had to try too hard. Swiftly, the reality would have sunk in. Railways were so much faster, and could carry far more. Canal freighters had to slash their prices, which led to the rise of a new community of water-borne families, as boatmen could no longer afford houses. By the 1850s the amount of cargo carried by canals had fallen by two thirds.

The evidence was there for those who could see it. In the 1930s Robert Aickman, who went on to form the Inland Waterways Association, wrote how, during a walk along the desolate canal north of Stratford-upon-Avon, 'Everywhere there were threatening notices, all stamped out on iron plates, and all in the name of the Great Western Railway Company.'

In many instances insult was added to injury, as the railways simply followed the path of the canals. The engineering expertise that had created the watery network had identified the most level lines to follow, so the railways were built adjacent to them. In an interesting parallel, many motorways now follow the paths of railways, which in turn follow the paths of canals – lines all leading the same way, as the newest threaten to eclipse the originators. The result was a decline almost into oblivion.

The only reason the Grand Union Canal is open to traffic today is the work of volunteers who have rescued such routes from ruin. If there is one particular person to thank for the salvage of the canal network, it is Lionel Thomas Caswall Rolt. Had this historian, author and enthusiast acted even a few years later, there might have been no revival of interest in these wonderful waterways. Change began in 1944, with the publication of his influential book *Narrow Boat*.

'If the canals are left to the mercies of economists and scientific planners,' wrote Rolt, 'before many years are past the last of them will become a weedy, stagnant ditch, and the bright boats will rot at the wharves, to live on only in old men's memories.'[3] Jo Bell has just written an introduction to the newest edition.

Such was the response to this poetic but unsentimental look at the fading light of water life that it led in 1946 to the formation of the Inland Waterways Association, and in due course to the rejuvenation of the canal system. The timing was fortuitous. At the same time as the IWA was being formed, Attlee's post-war government was setting up the British Transport Commission as part of the nationalisation of the country's infrastructure. Without the intervention of Rolt and his team, this would have seen the end of many of the remaining canals. It is worth bearing in mind that the last Chair of the Transport Commission was none other than the infamous Dr Beeching, and his axe might have fallen on those waterways had they lacked such important support.

Rolt travelled much of the network, finding some canals 'a shocking and lamentable sight, the more so as the dereliction is not yet fundamental, though it soon will be unless something is done.' And something was done – volunteers began to work on reclaiming mile after mile of these one-time motorways. In some instances the beds had to be dredged; many locks had to be repaired. Old skills had to be re-acquired by those fascinated in these neglected arteries.

While the arteries needed unclotting, they also needed to be detoxed. Canals running through industrial areas must have seemed like a wonderful opportunity for those wanting to dispose of irritating accumulations of toxic waste. And this is what happened to the Dudley No. 2 Canal.

Rattlechain Lagoon is a notorious spot in the West Midlands, and has been the focus of attention for residents for decades. Originally a clay pit, in 1899 it became flooded when the Birmingham Canal burst its banks. *NarrowBoat* magazine reported how some six miles of canal emptied, leaving boats stranded – and others, it is feared, swept away into the pit which was soon 100 metres deep. In the 1940s permission was given to use the pit as a waste-disposal facility, and for thirty-two years a totally unregulated dumping regime ensued. Such chemicals were in large part transported along the canal, and there were, inevitably, accidental spillages or even deliberate releases. And now? Mysterious deaths of wildlife have alarmed residents, and investigation has revealed some of this lagoon's highly toxic legacy – alarming amounts of white phosphorus, for example. The report from one-time Dudley Canal Trust volunteer, Roy Martin, who joined the team renovating the canal in 1968, gives an indication of the scale of the problem.

Most weekends for more than three years, volunteers dug out the black sludge that had settled over the last one hundred and fifty years. When we asked someone who knew more than us what was in it we were told it was a cocktail of allsorts from past industries. It contained heavy metals such as cadmium and zinc, and hydrocarbons of coal slack and oil plus other unknowns. It was nasty, and we nicknamed it 'the Dudley Treacle'.[4]

The water of the canal was often milky and sterile, and had the rather alarming capacity to burn if a cigarette was tossed into it. Roy described how specialist fire crews were needed to put out the flames. 'Boat ropes that had dropped into the water, were when dried likely to spontaneously combust, a known property of phosphorus, I have since found out.' Roy and his team could not remove all of the 'Treacle', so the sludge that remains was covered in a new layer of silt. Now the canals are blooming, but concerns persist as to what lies beneath them. As for the Rattlechain Lagoon – one hopes that the owners of the houses recently built nearby are aware of the area's rather grubby history.

This kind of polluted history from the West Midlands was what had so effectively informed my prejudice against canals, a prejudice that was taking quite a knock from my time out on *Tinker*. Environmental rules mean that unrepentant dumping of toxic waste is, if not a thing of the past, at least a far rarer occurrence. But we should remain wise to the words of Rolt: in *Navigable Waterways* he wrote that we live in 'a world of which we now have so much more knowledge and so much less respect'.

But the whole way we think about canals has changed. Quite how dramatic this shift has been I had not appreciated until Jo said, 'Try and imagine the M6 motorway in 100 years being used by pedestrians and cyclists for pleasure. That is how big a deal this change would be to anyone from the early nineteenth century. These were the motorways of the Industrial Revolution.'

Now, at walking pace again, it is time to let minds expand and see more deeply what is around us. How can we take in our world at 70 mph? The blur of light that approximates to the reality is all we have to go on, our brains compressing and approximating all the time. Now they can relax and absorb detail. Thinkers of the world recognise that walking is good for thinking. Wordsworth famously shifted into the transcendent as step followed step – the very activity of moving required that thoughts usually devoted to the background chatter of the mundane be overwhelmed by the needs of knees, thus freeing up the brain to wander.

I had always assumed that this was to do with the act of walking. But time spent on a narrow boat made me realise it has as much to do with the speed you move through the landscape. During one stretch on the Grand Union we had over an hour of plain sailing – no locks, nothing to interfere with the reverie that swoops over you as your eyes shift focus into the middle distance and your mind catches hold of ideas that walk by the boat.

Or you see a kingfisher. Then, suddenly, there is an electric thrill to match the flash of electric blue. I had been sat in the 'cratch' – the open bit at the front – mind wandering, when the lightning shot by.

I was trying to work out why I was being lulled and lured by the canal. These were, after all, the motorways of their day. Yet the Grand Union, which I had joined only a short hop from Birmingham International, was proving as bucolic a route as it was possible to imagine. It is a conundrum that L. T. C. Rolt contemplated – and also answered.

The engineers who built the waterways, he argued, 'were concerned that their work should make a positive contribution to the English scene'. Though he accepts that they were at an advantage to those that followed, 'A highway whose surface is a mirror of water finds a place in the landscape much more easily and naturally than do later roads of steel or tarmacadam.' The difference is more than just the medium. Rolt believed there was a fundamental difference – that the attitude of engineers towards nature has undergone a real change. 'As knowledge has vastly increased man's borrowed powers,' he says, echoing the messages coming now from some of the darkest of green activists, 'so his attitude towards the source of those powers has subtly altered. Whereas once he was concerned with art to direct, now he presumes with strength to command. What began as a sensitive and loving partnership has ended in a brutal and arrogant rape.'

This is the pivot on which our relationship with nature has shifted. As the canals grew, so the country loosened its attachment to the natural world at an accelerating rate. From this point in history linescapes became about our human connections at the cost of the fragmentation of the landscape.

As the dead roe deer we passed, swarmed with flies and lifelessly floating, attested. There are occasional bridges, but it is unlikely that wildlife will have read the map, so the appearance of a body of water will be for many an impassable barrier.

Most canals have an 'on' and 'off' side. The towpath will be on the 'on' side; that side will be owned and now managed by the Canal and River Trust, the successor to British Waterways, which took on the management of the canals from the British Transport Commission in 1963. It will also probably have been reinforced with metal and concrete closer to the locks. Which is why water voles will have more luck on the other, 'off', side – that side of the canal is a potential haven.

Jo was clearly quite concerned with the headaches that small mammals must receive from such reinforcement. As we gently chugged on I noticed a line of molehills following us. 'Yet more head-banging,' she declared. Normally a line of hills as straight as this would indicate a male on a mission to find a female, but this time there was another cause. I jumped out to investigate. A few hills were visible, perpendicular to the canal, reaching right up to the bank – and then they started to run parallel to it. For over 100 metres they were getting darker and newer. I could imagine the frustration of the determined worm-eater trying to go in the direction of its heart's desire, only to be perpetually thwarted by the robust shoring.

Yet here, in principle, was a perfect habitat for the wildest of watery mammals. I had to accept: this was as much otter country as the meandering streams of Devon. With that in mind I spent a fruitless few minutes inspecting and sniffing the molehills – otters frequently use prominent features to mark their territory, and the scent of their spraint is distinctive, some claim rather appealing.

To more fully understand what is going on in the world

it is often necessary to shift your perspective, and sniff a molehill. This was why having a crewmate like Helen was such a joy. She is a crime writer, which gives her a particular perspective, and as we travelled we soon found we were seeing things in rather different ways. I spotted a toad as I walked between lock gates; Helen saw a great place to hide a body. When we passed the dead roe deer, Helen made notes about the condition of bodies discovered floating in water. I found leaf-cutter bees nesting in the beam of a lock gate; Helen wondered whether the lock mechanism could be booby-trapped to become a murder weapon.

Meanwhile, Jo sat at the back of the boat, composed and composing, wondering quite what her crew were so excited about. And she really was composing. Her journey to Stratford was to take up her post as poet in residence for a month, coinciding with the River Festival at which she was to present a poem in her capacity as the Canal Laureate.

Now that journey took us across the Edstone Aqueduct, a disconcerting experience, floating over a valley for 145 metres. I decided to get an atmospheric photograph from the road below, but found the aqueduct path level with the bottom of the canal, which meant I was running along with my head level with the base of the boat. The aqueduct is only one boat wide, so there was no chance for *Tinker* to dally and pose for the photograph.

The aqueduct's steel structure was fascinating, covered in barnacle-like protrusions of dark brown rust, and at the waterline a pale stripe of residual salt. The information board I had a chance to read on the way back up explained how children used to learn to swim in this aerial pool when the canal was closed, and how canal water was fed through a valve at the base into steam engines as they stopped below. I loved the story of a fish causing a delay by blocking the intake pipe. Here was the canal clearly acting as an agent of connection, providing watery contact in a way the natural world could not, bridging a valley and crossing a road. Earlier we had done the opposite, going through a hill, under a road.

By the time we arrived in Stratford-upon-Avon we were all tired, and being back in an urban setting was a bit of a jolt. But that is the point of the canal: it carries with it a glimpse of wild. The looming presence of a Premier Inn as we scraped through and under narrow bridges set me imagining the people travelling to the same festival as Jo, leaving their homes behind to come and settle into their convenient cell for the night. I like to visit this gypsy world of narrowboats, but am not ready to embrace it as my own.

Suddenly we were in a basin beside the River Avon. Jo had a mooring set aside for her that, after a little jiggling around, we were able to claim. It was time for another cup of tea and a fond farewell. I had not expected to enjoy the canals as I did; my prejudice was seriously dented. Though it is also possible that the good company affected my objectivity. I unstrapped my bike from the roof and headed off to find the station, homeward on another line.

*

The canal is on the cusp – that point in history at which our ability to put the world to work for us changes gear and accelerates. From walking pace to outer space, the rate of change since has become exponential. We are the recipients of faster connections, greater consumption and deeper fragmentation.

At the same time the canal is both a brilliant agent of communication – just look at the riparian flora and fauna that relish the waterside life – and a real incision in the landscape, fragmenting it for many species. Rebuilt, repointed and re-loved, however, it is no longer the septic ditch of years gone by. Kingfishers and bats make it home.

This re-imagining of the canal is not restricted to the UK. The gradual change in the quality of water in the canals of the Dutch city, Leiden, thanks to good maintenance, has led locals to want to know more about what is in these gentle thoroughfares. As the water is cleaner, so the amount of wildlife increases. And the reason the canals remain clean is that the local population have become enthusiastic supporters of the waterways – because they are cleaner. It is a virtuous cycle, and one that brings a hint of wildness into the heart of a city. This is why these lines can be so important. They not only provide corridors for wildlife, but also bring a wilder life to where most people live. And this is in turn good for us; it makes us happier and fitter. There are 2,000 miles of canals in Britain, and 50 per cent of the population lives within 5 miles of one. There are more miles of canal in Birmingham than there are in Venice. We should start to treasure them, use them and prevent them becoming sumps again.

Bucolic or urban, canals are man-made slices through the environment, and while many creatures will be able to use them to some, or even great, advantage, there are going to be some animals that find them an obstacle. It is probably impossible to juggle the competing demands of all those who rely on the water – and the Canal and River Trust, which manages our waterways for both their wildlife and human inhabitants, has managed to upset many people who live on the water. For now, though, I was interested in how it met the needs of flora and fauna. Its chief ecologist is Dr Mark Robinson.

I met him at the Trust's Warwickshire office, by the Hatton Locks on the Grand Union Canal. And while he inhabits this office world comfortably, he has the air of energy and fitness about him that suggests his real love is not to be found behind a desk. 'While there are many animals and plants that obviously benefit from the canal network and all the riparian habitat it creates,' Mark told me, 'I think that they have a slightly less obvious role as agents of connection. Have a think about rivers – the ecosystem of a river is dependent upon the catchment area. You can look at the spread of wildlife along a river and much of it is beholden to that one catchment. But canals, well, they have the capacity to cut across catchments, providing linkages where there were none.'

Which can have its downside too, of course, as Mark pointed out. 'So, for example, if there is to be a more widespread release of beavers into the river network, which I personally think would be wonderful for biodiversity, the release would have to take place in river catchments not crossed by canals.'

Beavers have such a great capacity to remodel a landscape

that I can imagine they really could be quite a complication for a canal: canals rely on order; beavers create chaos. Though apparently the dam-building only kicks in when there is running water to dam – so having beavers around would be an additional incentive to keep the locks in order.

Could other wildlife present problems for canals? I'd been imagining moles and water voles bumping heads with the hard edges of some sections of canals, but most canals are more organic in construction – most in fact, lined with clay. So could a determined burrower cause mayhem?

'Unless we get beavers into the system, the only animals we have to worry about are badgers,' Mark explained. 'They can bore tunnels into embankments, and there is a risk that they could cause a breach. Which could be catastrophic: imagine the amount of water that would be liberated if one of the longer pounds was breached – that could be 21 miles of water cascading out into the countryside. Now, if it is just out into fields, we are less concerned, but it could as easily be a housing estate. So the consequences of failure are significant, and we do keep a very close eye on badger setts in and around embankments.' But, he reassured me, 'there has only ever been one break attributable to badgers, and if we know where they are we can monitor the sett. Clearly if it started expanding dramatically we could step in and, with the correct licence, move them.'

Monitoring the structural integrity of the canals is a serious business – each year around £15 million is spent just on that – and there is far more to worry about than just badgers. These are historical industrial artefacts that are at a potentially awkward intersection of organic and industrial processes. The water has its own set of rules that will help undermine the brickwork of bridges and the wooden gates of the locks.

Mark wanted to show me something, so took me for a short drive. We pulled onto the verge of a small road just beyond its bridge over the Grand Union canal – a bridge that was level with a far larger version that thundered just 20 metres away. This was the M42, a road I know all too well. Beneath it, enough concrete to satisfy a soulless architect. Concrete tagged relentlessly with graffiti, giving a slight air of colourful menace to an otherwise depressing and grey scene. We clambered over a fence and past a sign that said 'Danger of death'.

Water does not look its best reflecting the grey of a motorway. And despite the efforts of the spray-canned legates, the canal sapped the soul. My prejudice, so neatly dented by my time with *Tinker*, was returning. Except that when I paid a little more attention, I realised this looked like the same graffiti I had noticed on the journey with Jo. Luckily I had the same camera card with me and was able to scroll back and find that, yes, we had indeed chugged this way just a few months earlier.

Mark was unperturbed by this industrial scene. 'I became excited by canals around fourteen years ago,' he explained as we started to walk north, 'when I realised how important they are to bats. There is a tunnel under Birmingham, the Curzon Street tunnel, that is used by Daubenton's to get under some of the busiest roads in the country. Canals could have been built for bats; they provide amazing roosting and foraging habitats. Stretches of the Monmouthshire & Brecon, Kennet & Avon or the Caledonian Canals provide some of Britain's most tranquil and beautiful settings in which to watch them. From their point of view we have created a cross between Tesco and the M1.

'And it's not just bats. On the Swansea Canal you can find, if you are lucky, the rare fen raft spider. And look' – he stopped and pointed, as I too caught the piping song of a grey wagtail defending its territory under the thunderous road.

'Canals offer bats so much potential,' he continued as we ambled along the narrow towpath, occasionally dodging cyclists and runners. 'Bats have suffered because we have removed their food and their shelter. Farmland has become more like a factory, and the old trees, inside which bats would roost, well, they have gone too. But here, we are managing the canals with bats in mind.'

Emerging from another, but much smaller, arched bridge, I noticed the edges of the walls were scored deeply with many lines. Not just scratches: these were gouges 2–3 centimetres deep. Some were clearly home to spiders, but I could not see what had made them. 'This is a bridge from the nineteenth century,' Mark said. 'And those, they are relics of the age of horses. You see how we are on a curve in the canal here? As the horses went through the bridge and continued around the corner on the path, the rope was pulled tight against the structure of the bridge. If it was not for the arrival of diesel a bunch of these bridges might have been eventually felled!'

Beyond the scored bridge we reached the beginning of a residential mooring; a neat line of narrowboats with potted gardens, and one with unfeasibly white laundry drying in the autumn warmth. But what caught my eye was the water. A sudden change had come over it: a thin skin of scum was visible as far as we could see. Mark got down on the ground, dipped in a finger, had a sniff. 'Diesel,' he said. He got out his phone, took some photographs, sent them off to his head office and made some calls. It seemed likely the culprit was a fuel pump over on the far side. 'This is only the second time in all my years here I have ever seen anything like this.'

The water had not been inviting from the start, but the oil had given it even less appeal. Then came the first toy. Like a scene from a noir-ish detective thriller, the doll floated along face-down, next to a coconut. The Sikh religion requires the ashes of departed family members to be scattered on moving water, and for the Sikh community around Birmingham the canals are the nearest equivalent. They often place the ashes inside coconut shells. 'The water in the canals is not flowing as such,' said Mark, 'but there is always a slight movement, partly because when locks are opened, water is pulled through the system, and partly because they are not perfectly level.'

So the pink cuddly rabbit we came upon next, floating mournfully, was on a slow trip to London.

On the bank opposite the pink rabbit were vast rolls of coir, part of the attempt to maintain and increase the biodiversity of these waterways. 'We have a conflict in managing the canals,' Mark explained. 'Boaters would like hard,

144

vertical sides that allow them to moor up with ease and keep vegetation from narrowing the channel. But wildlife would rather have something softer and organic on which to grow. The coir can help reach a compromise. When we have a softer bank, then not only do water voles have a chance, but aquatic insects can set up home as well. These then become bat food.'

Hedgerows and treelines accompany much of the network, providing further habitat for bats and other wildlife. And the canals' structures add to the opportunities. For example, the elegant and dramatic Pontcysyllte Aqueduct near Wrexham is home to pipistrelles. Every five years they pull the plug on the aqueduct to carry out maintenance, releasing 1.5 million tons of water into the river below, but care is always taken to cause minimal disturbance to its residents.

Other structures don't have the nooks and crannies needed by bats, so Mark and his team, ably assisted by the legions of bat folk around the country, have been adding bat boxes and bat bricks (with a series of vertical slots in them, they look as though designed for ventilation, but are just the right size for a bat seeking a spot of peace and quiet).

Not all that flourishes in and along these watery ways is necessarily welcome, however. There are undesirables, like mink. This fantastically effective predator first arrived from America in the 1920s, for fur farms, but was not found breeding in the wild until 1956. Riparian specialists, they have since made a home on our canals and rivers – recently I got a beautiful sighting of one while swimming in the

Thames. But their beauty cannot compensate for the impact on many other animals that share their habitat, and the water vole in particular has suffered enormously. A few more otters would help keep them in check, but the most important way of protecting water voles is to remove mink. The author and academic Tom Moorhouse calculated that £50 million would get rid of them – a third of the cost of a single jet fighter. We just need to consider national priorities.

Other undesirables are less immediately charismatic. The American signal crayfish has almost got me eating meat again. Friends of mine used to collect them from the Thames with a double incentive: first, the meal, and secondly the thought that they were in some small way helping to remove a creature that not only out-competes our own crayfish but also, through its tunnels, causes the banks to tumble. The ecological reality is complicated, though. Removing the most sought-after large crayfish can increase the damage, as these individuals help keep the population as a whole under control.

When I first moved to Oxford I was taken aback during a walk down to the river by something that seemed utterly out of place – an adult terrapin sunning itself near the Iffley Lock. It had been there for a few years, and people had even been providing it with food to help it through the winter. Nor was it an isolated sighting. These reptiles were fad pets for a while when the Teenage Mutant Ninja Turtles were in vogue. Now efforts are under way to remove terrapins from the Ashby canal in Leicestershire. What starts as the size of a large coin can reach the size of a dinner plate, with a fondness for native fauna (and the fingers of the unprotected).

Killer shrimps, zebra mussels and Chinese mitten crabs have all stowed away and successfully colonised the waters of canals and rivers, and are now outcompeting and predating our native fauna. Certain plants are causing trouble too – my brush with the magnificent giant hogweed resulted in a massive blister on my knee and a trip to hospital. Hogweed uses the lines of canals to stride across the country.

Other invasives are less dramatic. The fairy fern and the New Zealand pigmy weed both are so greedy for life that they can smother a canal, blocking out light, which results in oxygen levels in the water plummeting.

Dealing with the impact of new species might seem a small problem, but after climate change it has been rated as the second greatest threat to Britain's wildlife. And the economic cost is staggering. One estimate puts the cost to the UK at up to £1.7 billion a year. This figure, from the former government agency, the Commonwealth Agriculture Bureaux International, has been criticised as being a gross overestimate, but even so, the CRT spends £700,000 each year treating invasive weeds alone. A single infestation of the benignly named floating pennywort can cost £25,000 a year to treat. The reason it is so difficult to deal with is partly down to the rate at which it grows – up to 20 centimetres a day – but also the fact that it can regenerate from even minuscule fragments.

To try and bring a halt to this kind of damage the CRT has been working closely with DEFRA and managed to get a ban on the importation of five of the worst species. Because it is the deliberate importation of exotic plants, by dealers who want to offer something new for ponds and fish-tanks, that is the biggest cause of escapes. The ballast water in ships is another important way organisms can hitch a ride to Britain.

Mark and all at the CRT are on constant alert for the next new threat. Because there are many more out there, just across the Channel and the North Sea. So far there are 134 established non-native species in freshwater ecosystems in Britain: mainland Europe has nearly 400 more, all of which could become a problem.[5]

Nevertheless, Mark's demeanour shows there is little that pleases him more than to be beside these slightly wild water-ways. On our way back to the car I stopped to look at the throbbing buzz of the hedge. There was a mass of ivy, and it was in bloom, its flowers attracting bees and hoverflies of many species. Ivy flowers, in small yellow-green clusters, are all too easy to ignore, but are just as vital and, if you take the trouble to look at them closely, as beautiful as any of the more gaudy eruptions.

So unassuming but so desirable, as they are one of the last offerings of nectar for the year. 'I think ivy is one of my favourite plants,' Mark said. 'The small flowers feed insects, which means food for bats. The cover, on the ground and on trees, provides shelter for insects, birds and mammals.'

A little further on Mark made an admission. 'You know, I don't really like canal boats' (we were passing a few at the time). 'Too claustrophobic for me – I would much rather get off and walk. And it is the walking that has made me understand, we should really care for these canals,' he said, with real passion.

He stopped and pointed, with some self-satisfaction, at the concrete edge of the path. We were back where we started, right under the M42, beside the graffiti I had noticed from Jo's boat. I followed his finger: there was a purplish black smudge. I dropped to my knees, lowered my nose and took a deep sniff. Somehow fish can metamorphose into something redolent of jasmine, tea, and maybe a hint of straw. Here, in the most unlikely of places, was proof of the presence of the wildest of animals. This surprisingly delightful offering was spraint: otter poo.

7

Railways

A journey by train proved to be the catalyst for this book. Looking out of the window brought home to me as never before the chequered character of our lined landscape. Hedges, walls, ditches, canals, roads and power lines – all connecting and fragmenting. But I had needed the time to look – to let the landscape slow down before my eyes.

What fascinates me most about the railways is that they actually brought about the unification of time across the country. Prior to November 1840 there were local times up to twenty minutes different from London's. Oxford was five minutes behind, Bristol ten. But railway timetables required unity, so the clock on the church was no longer society's guide; it was overtaken in importance by the station clock.

Travel along rails was not always so brisk. On one of my Dartmoor sojourns I took a brief misty-May walk up to Hay Tor. Because it is so close to the main road this is one of the most visited points on the moor, but it has a secret that is usually missed by those traipsing from coach to rock and back again. If you know where to look, you'll find the relics of an old tramline. It is no ordinary tramline, either.

Given that most of our relationships with trains are as

passengers, it is strange to think that we were largely an afterthought. Early lines were initially built for moving goods. The tramline on Dartmoor was laid out in 1820 to carry granite from the Hay Tor quarry 10 miles to the Stover canal. In time it helped to transform this solid land, with new cliffs that now hold a rainforest of ferns, moss and lichen.

The tracks were made out of the same material they carried; these silvery grey carved granite lines, sunk into the pony-cropped grass, guided me up to the quarry. They also guided me back in time. The air was filled with birdlife. Skylarks, fighting in song; stonechats chinking on gorse – even the blackbirds and robins: I could not remember, outside of a dawn chorus, so much life on show. Which then made me feel sad at the loss of abundance – bio-abundance – we are experiencing.

Back at high speed, travelling on a train one evening, I stood in the vestibule and took photographs of the sunset-rich countryside as we careered by. I had an image in mind: blurred foreground, something beyond expressionism and moving towards abstract, framing a still vision beyond. That very effect – 'optical flow' – had never been witnessed before the trains.

This speed enabled the railways to create new connections across the land, and for a hundred years they were a revolutionary force in society. Suddenly goods could be transported the length of the country in hours rather than days – though, like the internet of today, as production could become centralised this had the potential to rob people of their livelihoods.

Certainly the innovation was not universally appreciated: 'They are to me the loathsomest form of deviltry now extant,' declared the artist John Ruskin: 'animated and deliberate earthquakes, destructive of all wise social habit, or possible natural beauty, carriages of damned souls on the ridges of their own graves!' That here was a form of transport that would allow reading as you travelled might, however, help make amends. Now, though, we are as likely to have a view of an armpit as we are jolted about hunting for seats; surfing the erratic waves of delays. There are times when I feel a certain kinship with Ruskin.

But when you are lucky, take the time to look out of the train window. Enjoy the parallax and start to note the immediate and wonderful wildlife habitats you are passing through. Miles of un-peopled land-lines along which life can, possibly, flourish. And then have a think about what we have lost. While the 15,777 kilometres of railways we have now might seem extensive, in 1961 there were 28,100 kilometres, and more than twice the number of stations.[1] Smaller and quieter lines must have been even more attractive to wildlife.

Much of the land that was 'liberated' by Beeching's Axe was sold for development, often to ensure lines were never re-opened. But there are still wonderful stretches of disused line that have become part of an unofficial experiment in rewilding. There is an old railway embankment running along the bottom of a friend's garden in Essex that is as wild as you can imagine: badger setts, trees, and standing dead trees that are home and food to so much wildlife. If the farming and land management around the Ridgeway were to cease, it would not be long before a similar line of wildness evolved.

Other lines have been reimagined. When I lived in Bristol I would cycle to Bath along the 13-mile track developed by the transport charity Sustrans from the former Midland railway route culled by Beeching. The flat and smooth path is a treat in itself, and has the additional delights of artworks along the way. It is impressive for becoming an important commuter route at the same time as a fantastic linear wildlife habitat.

Sustrans has taken the task of reconnecting people seriously. Over 1,300 miles of former railways have been turned into cycle paths, and the network continues to grow. Gone are many of the obstacles people find to cycling. These routes are car-free.

It is a repeat of the canals story: once industrial thoroughfares, now lines of leisure. These new lines would startle the crews of the all-powerful steam trains. And what would the navvies who built the lines make of this frivolous use? At the height of the Industrial Revolution there were around 250,000 people building railways, and the tools of their trade were often just picks, shovels and wheelbarrows. A man who was expected to shift 20 tons of earth in a single day, and sleep on the floor of a rickety hut, with minimal interruptions for health and safety, might have found the beautifully levelled cycle path an interesting repurposing of his labour.[2]

Even on this rather diminished scale, the railway network

requires an enormous amount of planning. There are around 2.5 million trees growing alongside the rails; management of this vegetation costs around £100 million each year – and while there may be grumbles about the delays caused by work on the line, this is all done in the name of safety. In 2013/14 there were around 1,500 incidents of trees causing disruption, so it is clear that managing well is a priority if such problems are to be reduced.

The railway network has such ecological potential. But it is also rather tricky to explore. Special rules govern access to the railways – no longer are they a playground for children, and Jenny Agutter would probably be arrested for running onto the track and waving her red bloomers, however serious the threat ahead. Trespass can be met with a £1,000 fine.

So to get onto the tracks I needed the consent of Network Rail. They are responsible for not just the management of the railway itself, but also the 'soft estate', the land either side of the line that forms the buffer with the outside world. It proved to be a little trickier than I anticipated. But after a year of prodding, I eventually got a date organised with their ecologist, Octavia Neeves, for early June.

Dawn at this time of year has a beautiful crispness to it – the edges of things seem in sharper relief – but by 8 a.m., when we met on a small single-lane bridge in Dorset over the Dorchester-to-Yeovil line, the air was already hinting at the heat of the day to come. The view could have been from the 1950s; there was something almost innocent in the richly greened embankments that sloped down to the track. We had to wait for the safety team, so Octavia used the time to get me dressed up in protective clothing. 'Sorry', she said, 'all I could find were the water-proof PPE. Consider this an initiation into the world of Network Rail.'

As I did up the steel-toe-capped boots a van arrived – our security detail – and I was introduced to Cherelle and Nick. Cherelle was already out of the van filling in forms with a friendly no-nonsense air. She was, as her arm-band attested, COSS: 'Control of Site Safety'. 'Today I am his boss,' she said, with a smile, pointing at one of the most heavily tattooed man-mountains I have ever met. 'I will say when it is safe and when it is not safe. If I say we have to leave, we leave.' Nick's armband read, 'LOOK OUT'. On some people facial tattoos add a touch of menace, but there was a gentle calm about this man that marked him instantly likeable.

Cherelle's short safety briefing was mostly common sense. 'The rules are simple,' she said. 'We need to have 25 seconds' warning before a train reaches us. That should enable us to be in a position of safety for 10 seconds before it arrives. Here the trains will travel up to 75 mph, which means we need a sighting distance of 920 yards.' I was beginning to understand why there were two of them, and also why they would have preferred a third. So, if Octavia and myself have our heads down looking at something, there needs to be someone to warn us of an incoming train. If there is a slight curve on the track, then there will need to be someone further ahead to ensure that the 920-yard restriction is met. And if there is a steeper curve, there will need to be two other people to ensure that the flag-waving warnings get to us in time.

And yes, in this time of hi-tech, it is Nick's blue and white chequered flag that will keep us safe.'

Here, at least, there was no risk from a 'juice-rail'. The slightly raised third track that carries electricity on many commuter lines is a hazard I was glad not to have to worry about. However, the rails were a trip hazard, Cherelle went on, and the sleepers should not be walked on as they could be slippery, and the troughing channels were not designed to be footpaths, but we would walk on them when we could. 'And it is less of a problem here,' Cherelle added, 'but in some areas, near bridges, we have had a lot of problems with sharps – needles dropped by junkies. So please be careful where you put your hands.' The gate warning us of the £1,000 fine for trespass was opened, and I felt strangely apprehensive as we climbed down the steep steps to the line.

The 'troughing route' we would be walking along is the lidded, concrete channel that accompanies the entire network along which the signalling cables travel. Or not, as in this case there were three cables running alongside the empty container. We were not allowed to open the lid to find out if it was full, though: there is a web of 'tickets' that need to be earned to allow you to do different jobs. No one here had the right ticket to look inside, which was a shame. 'These are one of the secret wonders of the network,' Octavia explained. 'Newts hibernate in them, snakes hide out from the sun and loads of other reptiles use them for shelter.' Amphibians and reptiles were her big thing, and a Mars bar was on offer to the first person to spot either.

Walking along this occasionally wobbly 15-centimetre-wide channel was a wonderful experience, one I recommend to anyone who needs a good way to meditate. It required just enough concentration to stop from falling off to push extraneous thoughts to the side.

It took a few minutes to notice what was so obvious. Peace. This was one of the most tranquil spots I had been in ages. Chiffchaffs, chaffinches, distant dogs and clattering pigeons were all there was to be heard. The sun was still low, but its potential was clear. The banks were coated in rich green, in this section of mainly ash and sycamore. Octavia was noting anything of interest on her tablet computer. Animal paths were followed to see if they led to gaps in fences, or evidence of badgers.

The badger has a potential to cause trouble. The willingness of our largest remaining predator not to be cowed by humanity is getting it into so many scrapes. While a canal might erupt cataclysmically if there were to be an unfortunate sett dug, undermining the rails could be similarly disastrous. Digging under the ballast that supports the sleepers can cause the lines themselves to sag, forcing trains to slow down at the very least. 'Usually it will be an outlier sett that gets too close for comfort,' Octavia said. 'We get permission from Natural England to fence and exclude badgers, and in high-risk areas we can put down badger netting that will stop them digging.' So far all the paths we had seen were rabbits'. Railway lines must be a fox heaven, though we saw none.

Cherelle saw a movement and quietly said, 'Deer'. And there, 50 metres away, oblivious to us and his lack of correct permits, dawdled a male roe deer. He took his time, then looked up, saw us and headed up the bank. Along the rural lines fences are usually low enough to allow deer over, preventing them becoming trapped. In more urban areas they are higher to keep out the great menace. Us.

Nick's job was perfectly methodical. Every five seconds he had to look back, pause, then turn and carry on. I wondered whether this was just 'show' for me, so I kept a discreet count. Sure enough, he was absolutely, systematically, following his instruction. 'Train,' he said, calmly. And we all moved as far from the line as possible, backs against the brambles. As it got closer the others waved to the driver, and he hooted his horn back. When I used to visit my granny down in Broadstairs, one of the highlights, as we walked down to the beach, was to wait on the footbridge across the railway until a train appeared, and we would all wave and if we were lucky, get a wave and a honk back. Here, this was not cuteness: a one-armed wave tells the driver that you have seen the train and are not about to step in front of it. Two arms in the air are telling the driver to do an emergency stop.

I had kept my head up, wanting to get an action photo of a blurred train. The buffeting was impressive. I noticed that the others all had their backs turned. After the brief knee-shaker Octavia pointed out that their course of action came from experience. 'I have heard it described as a faecal mist,' she said. 'If someone is flushing the toilet on one of the older models you can see it emerging from beneath the train as it approaches. Really worth not being face on when that wave hits.'

A little further along the line I saw a patch of wild straw-berries. Vivid red against the green, very tempting until I remembered the mist. Also militating against a rosy snack was the evidence of fairly brutal management. In places the immediate trackside was bare of life, browned like a dog-pissed lawn. Herbicide trains chug around the network spraying a fug of toxins to help keep leaves off the line.

Clearly there is an important job that Octavia and her colleagues do in making sure that vegetation, in particular trees, do not fall onto the line and cause an accident. But the amount of ridicule the network managers received when the reason for delays was declared to be 'leaves on the line' was so great as to suggest to my perversely illogical mind that it was probably not true.

Turns out it is true, and definitely not as odd an excuse as you might imagine. There are around 30,000 hectares of land owned and managed by Network Rail, home to millions of trees and shrubs. In the autumn a mature tree can shed 50,000 leaves, which can result in thousands of tons of vegetation landing on the lines. So often does the issue come up that the company now has a separate web page dedicated to the problem:

> Compressed by passing trains, the leaves create a thin, Teflon-like layer on the rails, so train drivers have to brake earlier when approaching stations and signals to avoid overshooting and accelerate more gently to avoid wheel spin.
>
> Leaf mulch can also insulate trains from the rails,

with the result that our signalling system, which uses electric currents in the track to locate trains, becomes less accurate. To maintain safety, longer gaps must be left between trains, leading to delays.

In 2013 leaves caused 4.5 million hours of delays to passengers.[3]

The techniques Network Rail uses to counter the problem are fascinating, and confirm its seriousness. A fleet of trains cleans the rails with a sand-based gel; every autumn teams work round the clock descaling the lines and using citrus-based cleaner to loosen leaf mulch; they receive twice daily 'adhesion forecasts'; trains can spray ultra-fine sand just ahead of them to improve traction. I will no longer disrespect 'leaves on the line'.

And what of the 'wrong kind of snow'? Another much-maligned excuse.

It was first used in 1991, not by the then British Rail spokesperson, however, but by the media. As with the leaves, there was a truth behind the story. A particular fall of very soft and powdery snow had not been deep enough for blowers or ploughs to work, but still so fine that it got into electrical systems, causing short circuits.

And for the network, snow, when it comes, can be a real problem, whatever 'kind' it is. More than 30 centimetres deep, and trains need to have a snowplough fitted. Snow can also increase the risk of overhanging branches breaking off and blocking the line, while ice can work many forms of mischief. Keeping the network open is a mammoth undertaking.

In the past it was an easier job. More people worked on managing the lines, and were subject to fewer of those irritating restrictions that Cherelle and Nick insisted upon to keep us alive. Like snow and leaves, 'Health and Safety' has been unfairly targeted as the cause of so many perceived ills, when the main result of the increased restrictions on what we can do has been a decrease in the number of people killed or maimed at work.

In an earlier railway age, for example, the trackside environment had to be kept clear because signalling was done by line of sight. Steam trains did not need 'Herbie' to come along, as they scorched the vegetation themselves with sparks from the chimney. With the end of steam and the introduction of electronic signalling the need to keep the trackside bare disappeared, and many years went by before someone noticed that the trees had done what trees will do, and grown. Now there is a nationwide programme of moving all trees back 5 metres from the line.

But should wildlife be considered in this process? I know Network Rail is not a conservation organisation, but they are in possession of 30,000 hectares of land that is largely untouched, unbothered and wild. That is over half the area of the New Forest National Park. The network has the obvious capacity to be an agent of fragmentation – the deer we saw bounded free, but Octavia told me she has seen many badgers and foxes killed along the way. 'I have never seen a hedgehog killed on the line,' Octavia said; Nick agreed. 'The juice rail is raised off the ground so smaller animals can pass under it – the problem badgers have is that if they get a zap they will attack the offender, and that results in electrocution.'

As an agent of connectivity, though, the railways are famous. One of the most notorious examples began its story well before the age of steam. In the early 1700s Francisco Cupani and William Sherard returned from Sicily with an interesting yellow daisy that grew in the island's volcanic soil. A sample of this Sicilian ragwort was taken to the Oxford Botanic Gardens, from where it soon escaped, making its home in the stonework of many of the colleges. And that might have been it for the spread of this plant, had it not been for the Industrial Revolution. When the railways reached Oxford the now-renamed Oxford ragwort leapt out onto the clinker beds of the lines and began its gradual spread throughout the country.

> The vortex of air following the express train carries the fruits in its wake. I have seen them enter a railway-carriage window near Oxford and remain suspended in the air in the compartment until they found an exit at Tilehurst.
>
> George Druce, 1927[4]

So there was some delight on my part to find a single Oxford ragwort plant here, growing out of the 'four-foot' – the space between the rails. I had to get permission from Cherelle to step up and take a photograph, though in my new awareness of 'the mist' I was reluctant to prostrate myself to get the best shot. I felt remarkably vulnerable, head down, concentrating on things other than oncoming trains.

Sliding back down the scree of ballast I asked Octavia what drew her to this linescape? 'Have you tried working on the road network?' she replied. 'The noise, the smell, the sense of despair emanating from queues of cars in a jam? Just listen to this . . .' – and we paused. Even the dogs had stopped barking, and we were in a place back in time, when life was slower and the only twitter was birds gossiping.

That single plant was obviously the vanguard, breaking the path for its team, for soon there were pockets of ragwort alongside the track. 'We keep a note of all the plants that are listed,' Octavia said, 'so if I come across Japanese knot-weed, Himalayan balsam or giant hogweed, for example, I plot where they are on the system. For wildlife this is an unpeopled world – at least, it should be. There are not many places in the country that are as free from human inter-ference yet close to human habitation. And while there are some portions of the network that are pretty much as busy as the M25, just look at this.'

She was right; this piece of track was so peaceful. The three trains that we cowered from in the four hours we were walking were a small price to pay for the tranquillity. Though where we had stopped there was a background hum. I looked around for an electrical substation, but nothing but fields surrounded us. And then I noticed the bank of bram-bles. It was buzzing, the flowers heavy in bees. In a couple of months there was going to be a superabundance of fruit – no one would be allowed to collect it, but what a store for badger, mouse, blackbird and squirrel.

Cherelle was getting twitchy, though. However straight the

line might have felt, there were curves, and there was one ahead. And as there was only one Look Out we were going to have to turn round and head back. Before this outing I would have complained about Health and Safety 'gone mad', but now I understood the problem. For Nick to be in a position where he could see far enough around the corner would put him out of sight of Cherelle if we were to maintain the 25-second rule.

I was not too sad about cutting the day short. I had been trying not to complain, but my brilliant orange safety trousers had turned into a portable, localised sauna. While my upper body was pleasantly warm, my lower had disturbing rivulets of sweat trickling down my legs.

Despite the discomfort, this was a revelatory and beautiful day. Octavia talked about the work she was trying to do. Her mission over the week I met her was to work out whether there were any wildlife hotspots along this line, as there were plans to upgrade the signalling. This would mean a certain amount of disruption, with some small patches of green being lost to concrete, and she had the opportunity to highlight which bits must not be touched. I wondered if she could argue for keeping that beautiful hillside of bramble intact?

It was all part of the balance Octavia and her colleagues have to juggle. Network Rail's overriding concern is the safety and efficiency of the network. Yet it also has a responsibility, I believe, to manage the 30,000 hectares under its command with a consideration for more than just the bottom line.

As we walked back along the line, still with Nick keeping

watch and having to take occasional refuge, Octavia talked about some of the other wonderful wildlife that uses these railway lines. In a tunnel in Oxfordshire bats were roosting, and at risk of being struck by a train at either end of the night when they start to become active. So Network Rail had installed flashing lights that are triggered by the oncoming train, giving the bats time to flee. Being out at night to monitor them is not an option for humans on an active line, but static detectors work well, and around signal boxes it is possible to linger in safety to capture records.

Redundant railway tunnels are rather less daunting for bats. A few months before linking up with Octavia I had had a call from an old friend, the bat expert Huma Pearce. Knowing my interest in linear features, she invited me to join an expedition under London – to snoop on snoozing bats in the dark, damp and cold. Beside the underground station in Highgate were two pairs of disused railway tunnels. In the 1800s steam trains blackened the brickwork with soot, and when they stopped coming an even older trade took over. Now they were to be given their annual survey for bats.

We were met by Cindy Blaney, who had the job of keeping the small crowd of seventeen people safe and in order. Every year Cindy runs a hibernation survey, counting the bats that have taken refuge from the ravages of winter. Once upon a time the bats of Highgate and Hampstead would have relied upon the nooks and crannies of old trees, and then on the less-well insulated homes that followed. Nowadays, any nook will do.

It was such a bad choice of day – for the first time in ages the sun was out, and the bright-blue crisp sky demanded worship. In 1999 just two bats were found while the structure of the tunnels was being checked. This was enough to get people like Cindy to encourage what is now Transport for London to take an interest, and contribute to the protection of these delightful animals. She has been instrumental in changing attitudes towards these relics of a steamier and seamier past. There are now forty-six bat bricks and twelve bat boxes built into the walls of these tunnels, and the entrances are secured with metal doors (complete with bat-friendly grating), chains and padlocks. After enterprising self-obliterators dug under the gates, a concrete threshold has also been installed. Among the playing cards and the bits of discarded clothing, nevertheless, there was still the makings of a perfect tunnel cocktail: Stella, Strongbow and Solvite extra-strong glue.

At 300 metres long, tunnels like these are brilliant. The cold and damp are constant – important to an animal that uses cues in the environment as a signal to wake up. Smaller caverns warm up too often, disturbing hibernating inhabitants.

But would the enhancements have made any difference? Would the bats be using the bricks and boxes? The team of bat enthusiasts spread out along the pair of tunnels, torches dancing along the walls as well as on the floor, where the sleepers remained an irregular trip-hazard.

Bats are really quite small, and there was clearly a knack to finding them. Huma has some of the most refined bat-senses around, and can spot a little bundle of fur in the tiniest crevice or, impossibly, hooked beneath a peeling sheet of soot. Every now and then a pool of torchlight would generate a quiet cry of 'Bat' – I had been warned that whispering is not a good thing to do, as whispers have more ultrasound, high frequencies that can make even a sleeping bat prick up its tragus. While the droppings of pipistrelles have been found within the tunnels, Cindy was expecting to find just two species hibernating. Natterer's and Daubenton's are both from the genus *Myotis* – the mouse-eared bats. Daubenton's, in particular, needs water, and both are regular users of man-made structures like the dripping tunnels we were trudging through.

At that time of year telling one from the other was going to be tricky, as they would be secreted into the smallest crevices. When not hibernating, they are distinguished most easily by their echo-location calls – each species of bat has a distinctive pattern and frequency at which it shines the light of sound to bounce off potential prey. Now there was a lot of peering – and often a call for Huma to use her supernatural powers of perception. There was the ever-present risk of disturbance: torchlight can warm a bat, piercing its sleep with the hint of spring. At the slightest twitch we withdrew.

Three hours later we emerged into the sunlight, blinking like waking bats. Numbers were collated and we had a record – thirty-six bats – a great haul. And many of them were using the enhancements built into the walls of the tunnels. With a little care, these once smoke-filled caverns can once again provide a sanctuary for bats.

Whether in tunnels, along cycle tracks or beside a busy

commuter route, there is clearly so much potential for biodiversity along our railway lines. But while Octavia had been
a great guide to some of the life to be found along them, I
had to look to her boss for a more strategic view of what
might be made of this extensive estate.

Dr Neil Strong, the company's Environment Manager, had
recently written in a Natural England report that, 'We are
identifying locations where mitigation measures can help
improve both the resilience of the network and increase our
contribution to Britain's biodiversity.' Which gave me a good
feeling. Slowly, over the course of writing this book, I have
seen the challenges set out by the 2010 Lawton review at
least being considered seriously.

Neil and I had hoped to be able to meet out on the rails,
but time was too short, so we had to rely on a phone conversation. By way of introduction I sent him the photograph
I had taken of the ragwort on the line. He responded in
kind – with a fully ripe tomato growing in the 4-foot gap
between rails. Now that is a photograph that tells a story.

'First and foremost,' Neil said, outlining the absolute limi-
tation of his ambition, 'we have to get these big metal tubes
to arrive safely and on time. But that does not mean we
cannot make a significant contribution to the "National
Nature Network". That was the title of a report we commissioned back in 2013, and it had a strapline of "Putting the
lineside back to work", which is where the changes can most
easily take place.'

It is thrilling to see large land managers beginning to take
the lines seriously. The problem, of course, is always going

to be money – Neil may see the good that will come from managing the network for nature, but accountants will have a rather less nuanced metric against which everything is weighed.

'Look, in the harsh winter of 2013/14 we had costs of over £100 million caused by vegetation,' Neil said. 'It is always much cheaper to maintain the vegetation than to fix the damage when it is unmaintained. That is something the accountants are beginning to understand. But there are other numbers we can put into their spreadsheet that will make them pay more attention.

'For example, we can earn money from the biomass we liberate when managing the lineside habitat. The trees we cut down can be used as a biofuel. This all adds to the value of our work. And when managed carefully we mitigate the changes that are coming in our climate. If we are going to be getting wilder winters then we need to keep bigger trees in check – it saves money. We cannot expect everyone to appreciate biodiversity with the same level of sensitivity. Sometimes it has to pay, and if we can find the way of proving it pays, we are at an advantage.

'We have begun to shift the way we manage our soft estate,' Neil continued. 'We used to manage what was there and deal with it the best we could, but now we have a "green transport project", and are looking over the fence a little more, not focusing just on our long, thin island, but appreciating it in the context of the wider landscape.' This meant spreading this natural value out beyond the trackside fence.

'We have lines running through over 200 Sites of Special

Scientific Interest,' he explained. 'If we are to be true to a greener network we need to integrate what we do. We cannot work in isolation. So if we have a great line of sycamores, for example, but over the fence there is some precious calcareous grassland, well, everyone wins if we make a change in the way we manage our land. Removing the trees can seem drastic, but if we encourage the grassland to spread, well, we are helping the chalky soil erupt into a profusion of wild flowers. There can be up to forty different species of flowering plant in a single square metre of this endangered habitat. And to please the accountants, managing tall trees is hard work, so it ends up saving us money if we remove them and work towards wildlife-friendly grassland.'

Though it is not always easy to convince the neighbours that such a policy is a good idea. There are between 5 and 7 million people who could call themselves railway-neighbours, and many of them value screens of trees. Then there are the 1.6 billion people who use the network each year. Clear-felling never looks good, and Neil is prepared for the avalanche of criticism that comes his way. 'Of course, it is not just for wildlife that we have to cut trees. We have to cut trees back to keep people safe. It is not a good idea to have a forest growing up to the overhead cable, carrying 25,000 volts,' he said. 'But if there is a clear ecological gain to be had from changing the landscape more dramatically, then we will embrace that opportunity. We need to get rid of the species and habitats we don't want, and keep those we do.'

But still it comes down to safety. I was only buffeted by

75-mph trains: Neil has promised to get me beside some 'real' trains, travelling at 125 mph. I am usually up for a challenge, but this one really does fill me with a sense of dread. Clearly it would be safe, and with the likes of Nick and Cherelle in evidence I would know I was in the right place. But still, even at a station when a fast train is not stopping, there is something deeply unsettling about that mass of noise – like being on the edge of a cliff – knowing that one wrong step will end it all.

Keeping people safe can conflict with allowing the network to be a wildlife-friendly corridor. If the line is sealed off from the outside world with dramatic fencing, preventing urban incursions, we are back with the same limitations that got me agitated about habitat fragmentation in the first place. Wildlife will appear along those lines, but only wildlife that can fly over the fence. And rolling it out along the entire network is going to be very expensive.

In any case, most fencing along the network cannot keep out deer, and for night-time drivers, the dramatic collision with a large object can be a terrible fright. It might not derail the train, but they will be left not knowing what species was involved, and thinking you might have just been involved in the death of a person must be deeply distressing. Additionally, a large red deer stag can do real damage to a train – one managed to rupture a fuel tank, causing a massive fuel spill.

Aside from the occasional incident, the majority of the rail network seems a relatively benign environment. Yes, in the centre of great conurbations it needs sealing off from the most problematic of animals. But even then, there are places where you can see wild life sneaking into the heart of the city along these potentially barren lines. Rabbits will dig; foxes will get in. I have seen both looking in blank confusion at crowded commuter trains. Herds of people being rushed past calm observers.

Not all of the network is run by Network Rail. HS2, High Speed 2, the imaginatively named big brother of HS1, will carry people from London to Birmingham and beyond faster than we can imagine. But at some cost. The planned route will take out around 500 wildlife sites, either through direct destruction or by disturbance. These include ten SSSIs and 150 Local Wildlife Sites. In return? Well, this is where the entire world of biodiversity offsetting rears its very ugly head.

The UK government defines biodiversity offsets as 'conservation activities that are designed to give biodiversity benefits to compensate for losses – ensuring that when a development damages nature (and this damage cannot be avoided) new, bigger or better nature sites will be created'.[5] It is a concept that fills me with considerable unease. It does not take a genius to see where this theory falls flat on its face. Take, for example, the proposal to build a motorway service station on Smithy Wood near Sheffield. The developer offered to offset the loss of this ancient woodland by planting new trees and managing another woodland. Smithy Wood is at least 850 years old. At a stretch it is possible to see how an accountant, when presented with a spreadsheet of numbers, could find a parallel, but in reality? Or the staggering case of the UK's stronghold of nightingales at Lodge Hill, Kent, on which Medway Council decided to have 5,000 homes built. But they can offset the destruction, according to those convinced that nature accepts like-for-like as a good deal.

But what do they mean? Find 500 hectares of existing woodland and coppice it to become nightingale-friendly? What of the species who already thrive in older woodland? Maybe the offset needs to be offset – so find 500 hectares of field and plant it up with suitable trees. But if that area was available for offset, why not use it for the development?

Biodiversity offsetting is ripe for abuse. It can only be invoked when there is an accountant of some sorts tallying up the books; working out what value the threatened patch has, and finding something comparable to hand over to nature in exchange. For those values to be more than chalk and cheese, they need a common denominator, and so to allow for this sort of trade to take place requires putting a financial value onto nature.

The trail of destruction that will be wrought if HS2 gets permission will be enormous. Even if offsetting were to be meaningful, to accommodate the massive line carved into the countryside would require something remarkable and radical in return. But there is an additional problem, and that is the complete fragmentation of a great chunk of the British countryside. Unlike the relatively benign lines walked along by Octavia and her team, HS2 will be as hermetically sealed from the outside world as is possible.

The speed of transportation on such lines has accelerated beyond the dreams of the earliest exponents of rail travel. Fears in the early nineteenth century that travelling fast would make it impossible to breathe, or that our eyes would be damaged from continual refocusing, were clearly unfounded. Fears that these new lines will fragment the land have more grounding in truth.

Since the ice retreated 10,000 years ago, the pace of life for the majority of people on these islands has been walking. Walking pace – the speed of spring travelling from Land's End to John O'Groats (and taking longer when going uphill) – allows us to absorb what we see and encourages thought. But the speed we have gained in the acceleration of the last 200 years has changed our relationship to the world around us. It has removed us from nature as dramatically as the dawn of agriculture that brought us the reaves 3,500 years ago.

8

Roads

Modern roads represent so much that I find challenging in our relationship with the planet. The private car captures perfectly our inclination to be self-centred. With the slightest pressure from the ball of your foot you can generate such power. Power should come with responsibility, but the insularity of the car tends to generate a sense of entitlement – and that is where the trouble lies. Emboldened by such power we see everything else as obstacles.

This is not unique to motorised forms of transport. I imagine the stagecoach would have presumed a right of way over pedestrians. I doubt a gentleman on a horse would have expected to give way to a pedlar. But these days the power differential is so much greater. And the insulation of the powerful from their actions is of a different order. In a train, however much more comfortable your seat in first class may be, you will still arrive no sooner than the person standing in the toilet.

The origin of roads, as we have seen, can be traced back 6,000 years. By the Iron Age there was a recognisable network. It was the Romans who instigated a radial system – the concept of 'all roads lead to Rome' was something they took with them as they invaded – with the administrative hub being the place roads were linked with. There were far more roads than just the major routes, and what is quite remarkable is how long they lasted. It was not until the eighteenth century and the arrival of the turnpikes that Britain started to build anything better.

Turnpikes were toll roads. Tolls were collected along the route and the turnpike, the name coming from a defensive structure used by the military to repel cavalry, was the gate that controlled traffic. Prior to this it was the responsibility of parishes to maintain their own road network, but as long-distance travel and heavier carts needed better conditions this became increasingly impractical.

Roads have always stirred up strong feelings, as we shall see. The turnpikes were no different. Many local people resented having to pay to use routes that had been used freely for many generations. This was especially the case in the more mountainous regions where alternative paths were harder to find, and was one of the reasons for what became known as the Rebecca Riots in mid-Wales. Between 1839 and 1843, protesters, often dressed as women and taking a biblical injunction to heart, broke down toll gates. This resulted in reduced tolls for the community, but, perhaps more significantly, gave strength to the idea of a leaderless uprising, which was to be a key part of the protests against the roadbuilding of the late-twentieth century.

The turnpikes built on the network of the Middle Ages, and in turn became the guide for our modern roads, meaning that, as Francis Pryor writes in *The Making of the British*

Landscape, 'The layout of our modern trunk road and motor-way network would not have seemed at all unfamiliar to a Roman Britain.'

The scale, though, might prove daunting to an ancient visitor – there are about 246,000 miles of roads in Great Britain, around twenty-five times the length of the rail net-work and over a hundred times the length of our remaining canals. Other contrasts would intrigue Bronze Age engineers, however. They would have cut branches and laid them onto the boggier bits until the road was stable. Nowadays branches have been replaced by concrete pilings. Even today, though, some parts of the motorway network are built on what is known as 'peat porridge'. Notoriously, the area around Ottery and Middlezoy in Somerset has pilings that sink down 180 feet and still don't hit rock. Much of the M5 across the Somerset Levels pretty much floats.

My interest in this chapter is in the roads as carriers of motorised vehicles. The history of horse-drawn transport is an extension of the green lanes in terms of the impact on wildlife. The change that came with the car was profound. And not always expected. For example, when horses began to disappear from the streets of London, out-competed by the internal combustion engine, many bird populations suffered – those who had fed on the spilled seed from nosebags, and those that fed on the insects attracted by the horses' dung.

The shift was not all bad. The development of tarmac, the mix of bitumen and stone that created the metalled surface with which we are familiar, actually led to the creation of new wildlife habitats. It led to a narrowing of roads: un-metalled roads were often as much as 18 metres wide, as the rutted mud and extravagant potholes made travellers chart new paths around to the side of them. With tarmac there was no need for such width, and so was born the verge, an unintentional linear feature with great potential. After a slow start, by 1930 most main roads had this new surface.

Verges as linear features reach their apogee in Australia, where the 'long paddock' has been a feature of roads across the vastness. These stock routes were used to move sheep to market while providing them with grazing along the way. To prevent over-grazing there is a law requiring the flock to move six miles a day. And despite the arrival of vast lorry-trains to move livestock, this extended verge is still used in times of drought. Inadvertently, these lines have become havens for wildlife, providing both habitat and corridors for plants and animals.

For the most part, though, roads are set to ruin our natural world. There is the obvious carnage of dead wildlife. Up to 150,000 hedgehogs each year, along with 50,000 badgers and over 40,000 deer. There are possibly over a million vertebrates killed on the roads in Britain alone. In continental Europe it is estimated that up to 27 million birds are killed each year, and in the United States around a million vertebrates are killed on the roads *every single day*. And lest we forget about the financial impact of all this, in 2007 it was estimated that over $8 billion of damage to cars was caused in the USA from collisions with wildlife.[1]

There are attempts at mitigation. Froglife, the amphibian

and reptile conservation charity, has been running the effective and straightforward 'Toads on Roads' campaign for over thirty years. Toads are particularly vulnerable to traffic, having a migratory path to the ponds from which they emerged. Over the years, obstacles may form, and the journey to the ancestral pond become more difficult. But it is hard to persuade a toad, an animal that emerged from the late Carboniferous swamps over 300 million years ago, that the sudden arrival of a road is something to consider. Luckily there are thousands of people helping each year, with 'Toads on Roads', and between 1980 and 2013 over one million toads have been moved from the road – and the bodies of over 150,000 found. But despite these efforts, each year there are fewer toads on the roads, and since 2000 nineteen populations that used to receive help have become extinct.

The vast amount of meat laid out along the roads has become an important component of many scavengers' diet. Whether this provides a population benefit to scavengers, or whether the attrition of collision evens things out, researchers do not yet know. But the team from Project Splatter at Cardiff University have noticed far more buzzards appearing as casualties than their population suggests would be the case. Which is interesting, because their camera traps set up to monitor what was doing the scavenging show corvids and gulls as the most regular avian visitors. I imagine they are just faster than buzzards at getting out of the way of oncoming traffic.

Roadkill may not always be what it seems, though. I remember driving through Northumberland, doing a rigorous and exhausting research trip for *BBC Wildlife* Magazine on pubs situated in good wildlife areas, and being surprised at the fairly regular appearance of dead rabbits at the edges of roads. I mentioned this in the next pub, and was interested by the explanation. Gamekeepers kill rabbits, which is legal. But they want to kill birds of prey: not legal. So they take their dead rabbits and place them at regular intervals along busy roads, in the hope that cars will kill scavenging birds for them.

Road casualties play a rather gruesome role in helping us learn more about the state of some wildlife populations. The annual Mammals on Roads survey carried out by volunteers for the People's Trust for Endangered Species gives very good insights: the more dead hedgehogs you see, for example, the more hedgehogs there are in the environment around that road.

Less statistically rigorous, but impressive all the same, was the time I once drove through the night in Tanzania. As the headlights of our 4 x 4 swept the road its surface swarmed with mice and other small rodents scattering. Countless animals out at night on the road – I had never seen anything like it – yet I see no reason why Britain's roads should not once have pullulated with such an extravagance of life.

This depletion, or rather our appreciation of it, has got a name. It is known as 'shifting baselines'. The idea comes from the research into the fisheries industry conducted by Daniel Pauly – he noted how successive generations of fisheries analysts would base their ideas of a healthy marine population on what they themselves had experienced when they started work. Which meant there was a steady deterioration in the baseline to which they aspired.

In addition to road kill there is the destruction that comes with the construction of the roads themselves. My formative campaigning years were spent fighting the roadbuilding programme at Twyford Down – where the cutting for the extension of the M3 was slicing through sites of national natural and historical importance – and at Newbury, where the anti-bypass protests helped bring that round of roadbuilding to a standstill. The crudeness of a cost–benefit analysis that values a few minutes shaved off a journey over ancient woodland is deeply depressing. However many trees are planted alongside a new bypass, they will never be suitable compensation for the loss of developed ecological communities.

But the problem presented by our busy road network that concerns me most is its ability to fragment. Habitat fragmentation is a relatively unconsidered threat to the natural world; Lawton thrust it into the light with his 2010 report, ensuring that government had to at least take some notice. The irony that the lines we have built to connect have become the most effective agents of fragmentation, while the lines we built to fragment – hedges, walls, ditches and dykes – have all become the most effective agents of connection, is not lost on me.

The impact is not just on wildlife, but on us too. Human society, more connected than ever before, has in some respects never been so fragmented. Busy roads keep children inside, glued to sofas, increasingly unfit and with less connection to their community and the natural world. When you neither experience nor understand something – in this case community and nature – you care for it less. This then becomes a vicious cycle of neglect, destruction and decay.

An example of what is lost in surrender to the car came unexpectedly to me in Manchester, in June 1996. The IRA had exploded a murderous bomb on Corporation Street. Cars were banned, but cyclists could still reach the centre. I was working in an environmental and peace resource centre near the busy Piccadilly railway station. Taking a walk out at lunchtime I was amazed at what I could hear: footsteps and conversation. Yes, there was shock, but also an air of delight at the discovery of something long lost.

It should not take a tragedy to reconnect people. There are parts of the world which have developed road networks on a human scale, which act as thoroughfares for all sectors of society. In Copenhagen for a conference, I walked in to the centre and was amazed to see children playing on the side streets, and delighted by the serious provision for bicycles. Outside cafés at night I was at first surprised, then warmed, by the sight of bucket-fronted tricycles containing sleeping children, well wrapped in down duvets. Using the road network back in the UK my emotions tend to be frustration and rage as the whole damn thing grinds to a halt. I curse the traffic jam – and then remember that I too am traffic, and start to feel guilty.

Guilt was added to irony as I found myself on the Newbury bypass, on my way to meet the Highways England team, to hear another perspective on the roads, one they hoped would at least dent my prejudice.

Not all stories of the roads, to be fair, are of death and destruction. Giant hogweed has relished the rough land alongside the Westway as it staggers into London (though in recent years a herbicidal battering seems to have kept it from making the leap into Holland Park, Kensington Gardens and Hyde Park). Animals, too, have learnt to benefit from our road network. For a long time people have marvelled at the innate ability of the homing pigeon to travel long distances using magnetic and solar compasses. But more recently it has been found that they are also using our own (very human) road network. Researchers have followed them along the Oxford bypass, and watched them turn off at junctions, rather than take a shorter route by cutting off the corner.

As the relics of Hurricane Gonzalo buffeted my car, though, I imagine any pigeons would have just given up and stayed cooped-up at home. I was also feeling a tumbling in my gut as I realised I was off to meet with the people who have so long been 'the enemy'. But the agency was key to my understanding how the road network is managed. Maintaining urban and suburban routes (some 215,000 miles of roads) is the responsibility of local authorities, but there is something so assertive about the major arterial roads stamping themselves into the world that I wanted to know what was being done to lessen their impact.

The autumn leaves were set dancing by the squally winds, and occasionally they would lose a grip and let themselves loose, twisting in the turbulence of traffic and storm. A great swirl flew up in a flurry and turned into a flock of starlings playing in the wind. Vast stretches of verge and bank seemed enveloped in gauze as the furry woodbine swayed in its last days before winter.

Now I was on the A303 – a bit of a kill zone, it seemed. Maybe motorways are just so obviously unapproachable that less wildlife can get close, and that which does is left rather more unrecognisable than the sorry lumps of badger, fox and roe I saw clinging to the central reservation as I drove on to my rendezvous in Wiltshire.

Scavenging, mostly by wildlife but occasionally by an enterprising human, quickly removes a lot of the easier-to-eat meat. Even rarer are those who will turn the corpses of roadkill into art. Road-themed art may be fairly niche, but in 1996 there was a magnificent display along the 9-mile route of the Newbury bypass, as part of the protests against its construction. Called Art-Bypass, it consisted of sculptures, performances and installations of a beautiful and eccentric nature on the land soon to be lost to tarmac. More recently I was fortunate enough to see an exhibition called 'Soft Estate' in Liverpool's Bluecoats Gallery, by the artist Edward Chell.

His exploration has taken many forms. He uses photography, painting and video to capture images that pass us by, or rather that we pass by with so little attention. He notices and celebrates the unintended life that springs back in the face of our insult – creeping thistles and buttercups, foxgloves and cowslips that are captured in mysterious silhouette; hairy bittercress, dandelion and wood groundsel painted using colours of the roads beside which they grow. Reflective road signs hold the common ragwort, and number plates important names – Platanus, Larix, Wordsworth and Ruskin. A few months later I got to meet Edward in his London studio. 'The soft estate, the verges and other land managed by Highways England,' he said, 'is just such amazing space, so utterly unpeopled, and I was always careful and discreet in getting photographs that would simply not be possible from anywhere else.'

His obsession started in 2007. Stuck in a traffic jam on the M2 in Kent for hours, he got out of his car and went for a walk. 'I walked between the still cars and could hear flowers, leaves, stalks – all blowing gently in the breeze. A rustling murmur of unexpected life just begging for exploration. Some of the most unusual patches of flowering I have found,' he went on, 'are escapees from gardens and roadside shrines. I have found lupins and iris making a dash for freedom.'

The colours in Edward's work often come from the road. 'Look at these,' he said, taking me over to a stack of boxes in which jam jars were part-filled with what looked like dust. 'I always take a dustpan and brush with me, when going on a road-trip. Artists have always looked to the surroundings for material when creating images. Well, so do I. This dust is swept up from the roads and contains so many amazing things. There will be bits of carbon from diesels, there will be bits of rusty metal from old cars, and there will be highly sought-after elements that are always being ejected by catalytic converters. It's been estimated that a London road sweeper could collect £3,000 worth of platinum each year should they have the capacity to separate it out from the vast piles of other dust.'

.As I got ready to leave the studio I realised I had not looked out of the dimpled and majestically dirty windows. There was a canal right outside – I got a clear view through a broken corner of the glass. A coot created a wake on the wind-rippled surface, and on the towpath passers-by passed each other by without looking up. 'That's the Grand Union,' Edward said. My mind wandered back, north and west, to where the M42 crossed this same body of water. This line might be a barrier for some, but it is also a route right into the heart of the metropolis. It might be a push for an otter to make a home here, but one day Edward might just notice a pink rabbit floating by.

Back on my journey I was soon pulling off the A303 towards Salisbury on the Warminster Road and found my destination, the neatly presented if oddly named Pelican Inn. I felt rather apprehensive. Surely the people from Highways England would have done a little research into my background, and might take issue with some of the protests I had been part of?

I found the three of them sat at a round table by the window, and the big friendly bear of a man that is David Lovejoy announced that we could have a chat now, but I was going to need to be inducted before I could head out into the soft estate. For he was the Soft Estate Manager. I was introduced to the older of the two other men: quiet and clearly more senior, Tony Sangwine, Senior Principal Environment Adviser to Highways England, and then Joe Doyle, who worked with David for Skanska, the contractors who build and maintain many of our busiest roads.

I decided I might as well come clean, and explained how I had been at the anti-road protests at Twyford Down, Newbury Bypass and the Batheaston Bypass that cut through the iconic Solsbury Hill near Bath in 1994. If there was, as I think there should be, a map of the significant social unrest in this country, these places would have their own commemorative plaques. But David, Tony and Joe seemed unfazed by my occasional interference with bulldozers – if anything, my being so open made them warm to me. They were well aware, it seemed, of the challenges the road network creates for wildlife. What I was seeking from them was not a defence of various governments' love affairs with tarmac, but surprises. I wanted to know what the road network was good for.

The major roads Highways England manages represent just 12.7 per cent of our road network, but carry around 65 per cent of all traffic, and are where the most significant fragmentation occurs. Some wildlife can use our busy-ness to help navigate; other natural life can clearly march along the borders. But for the majority, these roads seem utterly incompatible with life.

As we began to chat, though, I found one of my earliest ornithological memories coming into my head. The roadside kestrel, once a common sight hovering in the wind alongside busy roads, sharp eyes held still as the wings flutter, waiting for mouse or vole to take a life-changing walk in the open. I realised I hadn't seen one for ages.

'Well, there has been a fourfold increase in the number of buzzards,' Tony explained. 'They have been outcompeting the kestrels.'

'But I think it might have more to do with the way we manage the soft estate,' interjected Dave. 'We used to mow one year in three; now we do it far less because we are encouraging other wildlife to grow – there are patches of orchids that would never have been able to cope with the old mowing regime. Anyway, less mowing means more cover for small mammals, so making hunting harder for a kestrel.'

I was rather pleased to see there was not going to be a dull and homogenous set of responses, as Tony now pointed out a problem with this more relaxed mowing regime. 'There has been a great increase in scrub invasion – along the M5 from Exeter, up to the M6. We have lost so much grassland to ash – that is one of our prime weed species.' Not that ash is having it all its own way: ash dieback, caused by a fungus, was first noticed in 2012 at a nursery in Buckinghamshire, and has spread rapidly. 'There is a balance,' said Tony, 'and sometimes it needs to be recalibrated with a pathogen.'

The conversation had been recalibrated too, and we were off on a depressing journey into the world of pests and disease. Dave talked about one species of the Fusarium fungus that has jumped from rhododendron to larch and now on to leylandii. Not many people would lose sleep over a little less of two of those, but I am very fond of the larch. As with the canals, the potential to be an agent of connectivity also allows roads to become a corridor for invasive species and disease. The ease with which we can now travel, not just from one end of the country to the other, but also across the continent, means we are always going to be close to a new disaster. I was too young to notice the elm going. If oak or yew were to follow it would break my heart.

The management of apparently similar estates can differ enormously, and the road team were rather critical of the railway network. 'There has always been a very different approach,' Dave said. 'For years rail's soft estate was just grass. But with the shift to diesel engines and electrical signals, the sides were left to grow. And now they use lots of chemicals and flails attached to work trains. *But* – they never do any stump treatment, so in effect they are managing hundreds of miles of coppice, stimulating growth.' I could see it made economic sense to go in hard and clear the ground, but might the railways' way of doing things explain why they offered such oppportunities for habitat?

I was eager to head out into the wilderness, but first Dave wanted to put his patch into perspective. He and Joe work in 'Area 2'; it sounded like something from *The X Files*, but was rather less mysterious. The road network of the country is split into twelve areas, and this one stretched from Tewkesbury to Exeter and across to Swindon, taking in chunks of busy roads like the M4, A303 and the A36, beside which we were now enjoying really quite reasonable coffee. Their 'estate' covered 2,122 hectares alongside 1,100 kilometres of road. This was no small patch.

Tony, meanwhile, talked about the changes in roadside maintenance, which, while disadvantaging kestrels, as we have seen, had correspondingly been aimed at assisting water voles. Around the M49 junction near Avonmouth water voles had colonised a ditch once its management had been changed. But if the money for such work were lost, so would the voles. Ash and other trees would move in. 'They are like hydra, these trees,' Tony explained. 'You cut them off and more just spring back up, so you have to do stump treatments. And we try to reduce the number of trips to roadsides, as each visit brings with it a real risk.'

It was a theme they kept coming back to. So many decisions made around the management of the soft estate were about keeping people out of the danger zone. 'This remains one of the most dangerous industries in the country,' David said. 'On average twenty-one people are killed each year.' Which is why my complaint about the concrete barriers running along the central reservations and slicing the countryside into ever smaller pockets of habitat, was given short shrift. 'We are putting these in wherever we can,' David explained, 'because the traditional vehicle restraint systems require maintenance. Every bolt needs to be checked for rust, and after an accident the cables need to be re-tensioned. And while we only do this when traffic volume is at its lowest, it is still a massive risk for my people. Concrete walls just need a broom.'

But it is not quite as simple as that. Subsequently I met someone else from Highways England at an ecological conference, who pointed out that the concrete barriers were there to stop vehicles crossing the central reservation – and were the only thing capable of stopping an articulated truck at 70 mph. As, of course, one would want. Though it is not without consequence: while a vehicle will be prevented from ploughing into oncoming traffic, it will be bounced back into the stream on its own side. And there is another real safety question, it seems, not being addressed.

So far there has been one confirmed death of a motorist hitting a wild boar. As these animals gain a more secure place in our countryside so the risks of encounters with cars increase. A concrete barrier down the middle of the road has the potential to trap boar, or deer for that matter, in the stream of traffic. And as the increase in road traffic is greater for nocturnal journeys, the risk of these animals becoming snared by these lines also increases, with catastrophic consequences. The only way to stop large animals getting into the traffic is to seal the roads off completely, which makes them even more complete barriers to wildlife. Unless, of course, the wildlife can fly.

It was induction time, and while the others went off to get ready, David ran through a considerable check-list before I would be allowed out onto the highway. It was based on an important yet often rare commodity: I would be issued with hard hat, glasses, gloves and reflective clothing – but as, with the railways, I would be expected to provide my own common sense.

The risks from vehicles are obvious; less so are those one can encounter in the soft estate. For example, missing manhole covers – they have been a target for metal thieves. Together with abundant rabbit holes, they can make exploring the undergrowth a little more risky. Then there is the rubbish. The instruction is clear: always wear gloves – what is thrown out of passing lorries and cars is about as unpleasant as you can imagine, and certainly rivals the 'faecal mist' I learnt about on the railways. And with that, I was taken out into the car park and presented with the brightest of clothing, the most uncomfortable of glasses, thick gloves that precluded any finer movements, and a large helmet.

After a short drive we pulled into a layby on the A36, and it was time to face the soft estate. I quickly discovered a new hazard: the safety glasses lent a slight alteration to my usual focus, so I walked a little as if drunk, tentatively lifting a foot and placing it deliberately in front of me. We started to walk along the strip of grass between the road and the trees, weaving through brambles and a startling amount of litter, a tideline of refuse from indolent motorists in harmony with the oily grime coating tenacious leaves and branches.

During winter the litter is at its worst. Not because there is necessarily more of it; just that with the absence of leaf cover it is more visible. Since that day I have been paying much more attention to the roads I've been driving along, and have been amazed at the quantity of litter. Cuts enforced by central government have had a real impact on the effort the road managers can put into clearing up our mess, and I wonder what unintended consequences this may lead to. I know when I visited Canada many years ago I was deeply impressed by the cleanliness of the streets, and imagine visitors to Britain would be shocked by such casual disregard for shared space.

More important is the question of how this casual abuse plays on our relationship with nature. If we, and in particular our children, see such little care devoted to the strip of green outside the confines of our car, it will inevitably inform and infect our deeper relationships with the world. We learn to be careless. I once drove behind a lorry shedding strips of plastic film into the commotion of wind. Such wraiths are not degradable, and catch in trees to become 'witches' knickers'. My passenger phoned the company advertised on the back of it, and soon afterwards we were pleased to see it pull over.

There are signs on slip roads entreating motorists to desist from littering. It is a threat not just to wildlife, either by consuming it or getting caught in it, but also to human life. Dave, Tony and Joe led me into this terrifying and litter-strewn linescape. As I was about to find out, litter-picking alongside a busy road must be one of the most unpleasant duties there is.

The rumble of traffic had me feeling anxious from the outset, and I found it hard to imagine anything with any degree of sensitivity could thrive in such an environment. Other than my guides, of course. Dave pointed out several small plastic rectangular boxes attached to branches at about chest height. He reached for one as it swayed alarmingly in the turbulence of another articulated truck. Inside was clear evidence of dormouse habitation. To me there could be few places on the planet as inhospitable as this roadside. But to the dormouse? Along this stretch the trees were managed so as not to become too big. And while many stumps were treated, there was also a great deal of coppice – perfect home for these sleepy rodents. And hazel, of which there was plenty, is a ready-made larder. Combine the lack of interference from people and the predator deterrence provided by the tumultuous cacophony, and you have dormouse heaven. They have even been found along central reservations and on roundabouts. Which calls into question the assumption that dormice never cross open space.

Knowing that dormice could tolerate this onslaught did little to ease my own anxiety, so I was pleased to be led into the deeper recesses of the soft estate. We were near the apex of a triangle of land. A railway line to our left, the A36 to our right, and 400 metres ahead another road, this patch was largely wild – probably as much of a wilderness as it was possible to walk in around there. Very quickly we were lost in a tangle of mature, untouched woodland. Occasionally there was evidence of human involvement, the vestiges of a track that must have led away from an earlier incarnation of the A36. There were trees of real size and presence, magnificent hemlocks that belied the natural feel of this woodland.

Down here away from the road all sense of urgency had vanished, along with any expectation of meeting another soul. 'Though sometimes you will meet someone,' Tony said. 'I remember there was a patch of woodland like this, and one of our teams found someone living in a makeshift camp. They were clearly not wanting the benefits of society, just needing to be alone. So we just asked that he keep the place tidy. He took that to heart and spent his days filling sacks of litter that had been strewn by less caring motorists.'

There are occasions when I wish I could get out and explore the central reservations along motorways. There is a stretch of the M40 north of Banbury where a series of rich-looking woodland patches are so very inviting; vibrant undergrowth that hints at great diversity. They must also be some of the most unpeopled woods in Oxfordshire.

As wild and potentially wonderful as these unlikely wildernesses are, they mask the inevitable fragmentation. Here was an opportunity to talk about the reality of reparations. Could these obviously ecologically aware men not influence the powers that be? 'The trouble we face is that we have to spend our lives dealing with engineers,' Tony said. 'They live in a world of concrete, steel and tarmac and they really struggle with the infinite variability of nature. We are keen not to come across as the people who just cause trouble, but we do need to educate many others within the agency.'

Another scary walk along the verge back to the car, and by the time we had said our goodbyes back at the pub car park I was deep in thought, my prejudices radically challenged. To many creatures, including me, roads are a nightmare of swift death or slow decline in isolated pockets. Yet they also have the potential to provide corridors and sanctuary for life. Especially if managed with that in mind.

Sometimes the life that thrives along such lines is not the result of careful management. The stream of litter is not the only recent arrival. In March and early April over the last few years I have been noticing a dirty-white blur on the verges of major roads. It took a while to register the change that was taking place in the first foot of dry land next to the swirling tarmac sea. Only when I stopped the car in a layby on an Oxfordshire road and went to investigate did I see what was really going on. A small, very pale, pinkish flower set amongst slightly succulent leaves seemed to have become a rampant addition to the network.

The person to speak to was Dr Trevor Dines, a botanist who works with the conservation charity Plantlife. The plant I had noticed is extraordinary, he explained. Called Danish scurvygrass, it is a brassica, related to cabbage, so not a grass and probably not Danish. I had assumed with a name like that this was yet another of those invasives, but it seems likely this plant has had an unassuming existence hugging the coastline of Britain for 10,000 years, since the retreat of the last ice age. So why was I only noticing it now? And what was it doing about as far from the coast as is possible to get? The speed at which it has charged around the country is astounding. Trevor had done some calculations. 'In Worcestershire we noticed the plant was spreading,' he said, 'at around 30.5 kilometres a year. That is 3.5 metres an hour.' I had read that snails move at one metre an hour.

The plant got its name from the large amounts of vitamin C to be found in the leaves – and these leaves were found by sailors, in the days before we understood the importance of vitamin C, to be good at alleviating the symptoms of scurvy. That the plant is beneficial to human health is a side-effect of its ability to tolerate the salty margins of the land. When salt gets into a salt-intolerant plant it sets off a reaction that results in free radicals being released which cause even more damage. Vitamin C mops up free radicals, enabling this amazing plant to carry on living in conditions most find intolerable.

Now it becomes clear why this plant has spread. Each year

we are applying some 2 million tons of salt to British roads. We are re-creating the inhospitable landscape of the very shoreline of the land in thin strips right across the country, leaving them as salted as a Christmas ham. Over 80 per cent of our wild flora cannot tolerate any salt at all, let alone the levels found in these toxic strips, so as soon as the leap was made from coast to road, the spread was inevitable. The speed of its spread has been in large part thanks to the turbulence of our car-borne lives. Passing cars whip up storms of wind, which lift the seeds and assist their progress at a rate to leave molluscs jealous.

Scurvygrass is not alone in finding these inland seasides attractive. Trevor told me to look for reflexed saltmarsh grass, grass-leaved orache and buck's-horn plantain as others now favouring our verges – though I am tempted to think he chose those just to show off the amazing names. The one I liked most was the prickly lettuce. While looking remarkably unlike ordinary edible lettuce, it is a close, if bitter-tasting, relative. The real magic of the plant, though, is acknowledged by its alternative name, the 'compass plant'. The leaves point east–west to avoid the drying action of midday sun.

Here are roads, then, acting not as barriers but as corridors – but should we be welcoming of species as they move into previously unvisited corners of the countryside? There has been a great deal of discussion; recently, in his new book *The New Wild*, the writer Fred Pearce has suggested we embrace the arrival of the new. For the most part, nature welcomes new arrivals; it is only people, who try to manage nature, who find this difficult. Pearce's work requires us radically to reconsider our whole relationship with the world.

The very thin and poor-quality soil of the roadside is perfect for the sorts of flowering plants that have disappeared from the vast majority of the countryside – at least 97 per cent of wildflower meadows have been destroyed since the end of the Second World War. By fertilising the land and sowing it with crops like perennial rye the rich variety that once flourished has been swept aside. So these strips of land beside our roads are refuges for what was once commonplace, their value increasingly recognised not just in the obvious aesthetic delight that comes with a swathe of flowers, but also the understanding of how important this variety of species is to the bee community.

So it is a shame, just when the verges of Britain are becoming an unexpected home to new coastal species, that their potential is being completely undermined by absurd management. The author Mim Darlington tweeted a lovely picture as she travelled between Dartington and Buckfastleigh in Devon, of orchids running a riot of delight along the roadside, weaving their way among other floral flourishes. Yet on her return journey that same day, the verge had been shaved, stripped of the colour and the pollen-rich plants.

She is not alone in noticing such crimes against nature. Councils throughout the land are being lobbied by Plantlife, and some are turning to the light, embracing nature and, if they are clever, saving some money too. Another conservation group, Buglife, has launched the 'B-Line' campaign, to create a network of flower-rich pathways across both urban and rural areas. The county council in Dorset is in the vanguard of joined-up thinking, and has been recognised as particularly committed to helping its verdant verges. It is doing more than just leaving them alone; it is investigating management regimes that will lead to reduced soil fertility, which in turn leads to reduced grass growth, and less need to mow. On some roadsides the topsoil has been stripped down to less fertile subsoil, or even rock. Mini hay bales are harvested where possible, as this removes the fertility from the verge. Yellow rattle has been sown, which attracts bees and can subjugate grass. In some broader verges sheep have been brought in, enabling the council to reproduce traditional meadow management. And finally, rather than leaving the grass cuttings to compost down along the roadside, keeping the fertility in, they are being removed and taken to biomass generators to produce electricity. Money will be saved and wildlife will benefit.

But for the most part wildlife will not benefit. These lines remain something resting on, or cutting through, a once more natural landscape; and wildlife will have had to make way. The roads may not have become complete wastelands – but the corpse count indicates their success as a barrier to free movement.

The barrier is more insidious than the dead bodies suggest. Radio-tracking shows that hedgehogs tend to veer away from, rather than attempt to cross, very busy roads. This means that the land is being fragmented to an even greater extent. Fragmentation can have a profound impact on a species' ability to thrive. We now know that hedgehogs need at least 90 hectares to maintain a viable population. That is around three 18-hole golf courses of contiguous area – and that presumes only the best quality habitat. For the semi-industrial wasteland that is much of our rural landscape the requirements are far greater: nearly 4 square kilometres.

It is not just the landlubbers who get stuck when the roads get bigger and busier. Some bats, such as the pipistrelle and noctule, actively choose minor roads to feed along, especially when bordered by hedges (Natterer's actively avoid all roads). On the kind of corridors managed by Highways England, though, it has been found that bat activity and diversity increases threefold as you move away from the road. Dutch research found that bats were massively affected up to a kilometre from the road. Mitigation work in the Netherlands has concentrated on establishing 'hop-over' sections that encourage bats to fly at least 5 metres above the road surface, keeping them out of the way of large lorries and the turbulence they bring. Unfortunately, it seems that the bats have not been reading the manual, and are still being hit by trucks as they swoop down into their path.

The disturbance to birds is not just from collisions. An experiment was conducted in Idaho, USA, in which a 'phantom road' was created, with speakers broadcasting the noise of a highway. The researchers found a 25 per cent reduction in bird abundance and a complete absence of some species, when compared to a control site. Given that 83 per cent of that massive country is within a kilometre of a road, you can see how widespread the problem has become.

Globally, the situation is highlighted most alarmingly by recent research revealing that roads have fragmented the earth's remaining untrammeled land areas into 600,000 pieces, most of which are too small to support significant wildlife.

In Britain we love the song of our garden birds, even if often they just signify a pretty way of fighting. But how has the steady drone of rubber on tar, combined with the growl of engines and the wailing of sirens, affected their ability to communicate? It seems such noise can mask the lower tones of birdsong, and this affects the ability of a female to assess the quality of a potential mate. To counter this, birds have been found to sing at a higher pitch to try and rise above the cacophony. This in turn affects the chances of urban males winning over rural females, setting up a different fragmentation in the population. Additionally, traffic noise can prevent a bird hearing an approaching predator or finding prey, if sound is one of its customary cues.

Just because there is a barrier does not mean that wildlife will not try and cross. The ecological consultant Jochen Langbein estimates there are around 70,000 deer casualties each year on the UK's roads, causing many hundreds of human injuries and several fatalities. Yet on the outskirts of many major cities nowadays there are deer that will have had to cross motorways. Jochen and a colleague set up camera traps to investigate how they managed it. They found the deer were using both bridges and underpasses, walking quite calmly. On smaller roads, however, deer just take their chances. And as videos Jochen has collected over the years show, if you see a deer dart across the road in your headlights, slow right down. It may well be just the vanguard. More might follow. The best way to keep deer off motorways is with high, deer-specific fencing, which works most effectively if it funnels the deer towards a suitable crossing. But this then further fragments the environment for other wildlife.

Trying to manage nature is never going to be easy. We can work hard to help one species, only to find this impinges on another. Wildlife protection legislation, for example, demands that great crested newts are treated with the utmost care, including the use of 'newt fencing' to exclude them from areas of disturbance. This plastic wall, buried slightly to prevent burrowing, has the unintended consequence of preventing other wildlife from free movement.

It is almost impossible to imagine our roads being managed with wildlife in mind. Then again, I'm sure it would have been impossible for the canal workers of the nineteenth century to imagine how these waterways are used now. Could roads be transformed in form and function into linear features that connected both us and the wildlife they currently disturb?

There are moments, on some of the quieter tarmac lines, when wildlife's ability to see beyond the obvious impediment of the road gives me hope. Next time you see pied wagtails bobbing their rears up and down a road, have a think as to why. Usually they would act out this dance alongside a river – the wagging motion, like that of the dipper, acting as a camouflage, disrupting their shape and allowing them to hide in plain sight of potential predators. Like so much wildlife, they have co-opted our intrusion and made it their own. The road is just another linear feature for the wagtails to patrol, looking for insects. Though it is a rather less hospitable environment for invertebrates, they are there, attracted by the warmth stored in the black stuff.

There is no escaping roads; not for us, not for wildlife. These man-made arteries, often clogged, have revolutionised our lives as did the canals and the railways before them. But their potential to fragment is in a different league.

Yet, if we are willing to shift our perspective, it is possible to start seeing roads in a different light, and recognise them as a potential good. Remember that the canals, now largely wonderful for wildlife, were once the highways of their time. If we can use the roads less, encourage their managers to fertile innovation, and be brave with investment, then wildlife might just have a chance.

9

Pylons and Pipelines

The great steel giants that stride across the land like conquering robots from a 1950s sci-fi B-movie are so much of our lives that they – almost – blend into the landscape. But these pylons and their cable cargo make a surprising contribution to the nation's linescape.

These lines, the high-voltage system, are managed by the National Grid. Around 7,000 kilometres of overhead lines and 600 kilometres underground, they are the power equivalent of the motorways. They carry electricity at 275,000 volts to large substations, those slightly ominously fizzing and buzzing developments usually on the edge of built-up areas, inside which the voltage is 'stepped down,' through a series of oil-filled transformers, to 22,000 volts – and there ends the responsibility of the National Grid. The electricity then heads back out, and on to us, using the rest of the network – the A, B and unclassified roads, to continue the metaphor – under the control of the power companies we have come to love or loathe.

It might seem that these are the most benign of lines, to wildlife at least. Floating above the ground, their ability to fragment the landscape is, at first look, negligible. Buried beneath the ground, they must be even more innocuous. But there are very real issues, some of which are only just being understood.

It has long been noticed that mammals and ground-nesting birds avoid a considerable area around high-voltage power lines – in some instances a range of several kilometres. This is perplexing: these lines are neither impenetrable physical barriers nor associated with human traffic. More perplexing still, this barrier effect continues for decades, suggesting that the animals do not become acclimatised. Which in turn means that whatever is causing the problem is being reinforced.

Dr Nicholas Tyler of the Arctic University of Norway has been investigating one particular problem. 'We have known for a long time that reindeer avoid power lines,' he told me. 'Reindeer herders periodically try and sue the power compan-ies for the fragmentation of their land, but there has never been any empirical evidence they could use. Well, now we have changed that.' Nicholas and his team have come to a startling revelation. They have examined the eyes of reindeer, and found that these animals see ultraviolet light. This is a shorter frequency of light than we normally see. And it is the 'invisible' light that is given off by high-voltage cables.

There are particular reasons why reindeer are sensitive to this kind of light. During the winter in reindeer's northern habitats there are around four months of darkness. As a result the animals' eyes have become very sensitively adapted to the dark, able to pick up the stray photons and process them for information about danger. One of the signals of danger is movement. On power lines this ultraviolet light can flash in such a way as to suggest movement, therefore frightening the reindeer. The random nature, in both time and space, of these flashes makes it impossible for the reindeer to acclimatise to them.

A recent paper published by the Royal Society widens the issue: 'The spectral transmission of ocular media suggests ultraviolet sensitivity is widespread among mammals.' We don't know yet how this translates into their reactions to the light, but it is clear many more species can see UV light than previously thought.

Other animals are affected by power lines, though not always in an obvious way. While reindeer actively avoid such lines, moose, for example, exploit them. 'Moose are a forest ungulate,' Dr Tyler explained. 'One habitat they actively seek out is clear-cut' (in other words, the straight swathes cut through forest or brush for a line of pylons), 'as this is where they will find the new growth of low vegetation they love. And Arctic foxes are known to spend a lot of time under power lines too – though this is because of another of the more negative impacts they have.'

Nick explained how birds – ptarmigan and other grouse-like birds in particular – are regular casualties from collision: it has been estimated that around 50,000 are killed a year in Norway alone. Interestingly, in several countries there has been an attempt to calculate the impact power lines have on birds. In Canada researchers estimated that between 2.5 and 25 million birds were killed each year – and in the United States 175 million – in collisions with power lines. The foxes are attracted in turn by the opportunity to scavenge the unfortunate victims. These may be passive lines, but they are certainly not benign.

Perhaps surprisingly, ptarmigan see UV really clearly, which would suggest they would be able to avoid trouble. But these high-voltage lines have three cables; two are live, and one earth. The earth cable does not glow; it has no corona. And it is into this cable that the poor birds are flying. They are avoiding the light wall, and crashing into the invisible line.

Being killed in a collision with power lines is an obvious problem, and so is having a habitat fragmented. But recent thinking suggests something even more worrying. In the journal *Trends in Ecology and Evolution* Keren Raiter from the University of Western Australia has undertaken a review of what she calls 'enigmatic ecological impacts'. I am interested in two in particular. The first is, as we have seen, when animals respond to something that is outside the range of normal human senses, like the UV corona on power lines. This is known as cryptic disturbance. The second is called piecemeal disturbance: trivial disturbances, none of which amount to a significant problem on their own, but which combine into something far bigger than the sum of their parts. For example, there is the noise generated by the power line, the disturbance caused by maintenance vehicles, the clearance of vegetation beneath the lines, and an increase in predator activity induced by the open space. Piecemeal disturbance is almost impossible to quantify, but of potentially enormous consequence.

Now I want to look further at the problem of actual collisions.

Birds have a fantastic capacity to navigate great swaying obstacles that potentially obstruct flight. That they do not spend all their time being clobbered by trees has made me a little suspicious of the claims that man-made features cause many casualties. But if the figure for numbers of birds killed in the USA is even remotely accurate, there must be some sort of problem. So why don't birds just fly around the power lines?

To start with, 'birds' is a very disparate grouping. Different species share many features, but that does not make them all the same. Some react and behave differently to others. Some birds seem pretty immune to power lines, others less so – and for good reason.

Birds are killed in two ways by these lines. Obviously, collision is one of them. In bad weather and poor visibility, like fog, cloud and heavy rain, power lines can be pretty much invisible. Add to this a high wind reducing manoeuvrability and the risk is plain to see, even if the wires are not. Even the most agile of birds is not immune in these conditions. My memory is scarred by having had to dispatch an Arctic tern in front of a school group up in Orkney. These amazing birds can manage an annual round trip of 70,000 kilometres as they migrate; yet this one had been caught in a squall and hurled into the island's only power line, all but severing a wing.

The problem is not insurmountable. You may have noticed, especially around estuaries, that power lines are sometimes slung with what look like marine buoys. These are to make the wires more visible to larger birds like geese and swans.

Less easily soluble is the problem of electrocution. It is not a threat to all birds: it is really only the biggest, the ones with a wingspan that can bridge the gap between two cables, or a cable and the pylon tower, thus completing a circuit and becoming an unwilling resistor within it. A large bird collision can take out the wire altogether and cause power outages. In drier climes there is the real and unfortunate risk of electrocuted birds actually catching alight, falling to the ground and starting bush fires. Fortunately this sort of thing tends to happen only with poorly maintained or badly designed cabling.

For a better understanding of how Britain's power lines are managed I arranged to meet Ian Glover at the National Grid's head offices just outside Warwick. While his background was in molecular biology, he was able to explain why the cables I had come across in Devon, while nervously radio-tracking hedgehogs beneath them, had been crackling and glowing so much. New ones, he explained, are much more prone to this than older ones, and it was because of their smooth surface. 'You know how water beads up on the paintwork of a new car? Well, these droplets, standing proud on smooth cables, are being stretched by the fluctuating current fifty times a second. And the noise comes from the snapping of these droplets as they pop between stretched and relaxed forms. And as for you? We keep the lines a minimum of 7.3 metres above the ground, so unless you were a lot taller back then, I think you were pretty safe.'

As we talked, it was interesting to realise that the challenge the Grid faces is not just to protect wildlife from power lines, but also to protect the lines from wildlife. In a landscape that may have lost many of its old trees, these structures are attractive to some roosting and nesting birds, and especially to the kind of birds that tend towards the more dramatic nest designs. The National Grid has licences from Natural England enabling it to 'manage' interfering nests in an emergency.

Roosting starlings are a particular problem, and when starlings decide it is time to party, they can party big-time. Anyone who has found themselves underneath such an accumulation of birds will know the real problem: droppings. Starling droppings can increase the light and noise generated by the cables, as any irregularities in the conductor surface will increase the intensity of the coronal discharge. But getting rid of thousands of starlings is not easy. Dummy owls with moving heads have had some success, but the best solution comes in the form of pneumatic knockers. Starlings hunt for food in part using their sensitive legs to pick up the vibrations of their prey beneath the earth. This sensitivity makes them less happy to roost on a tower that is being tapped at irregular intervals by pneumatic knockers.

For most people, however, the issue with a line of pylons across the land is aesthetic. This linescape rises up above the landscape and, however conditioned we have become by constant exposure, can still cause its own kind of electric jolt. In some instances the answer is subterranean. 'We are putting some cables underground, but it is far more expensive and also can be massively disrupting,' Ian explained. 'For example, the London Power Tunnels are some of the biggest being excavated in the city. We are going underground there because it is just not practical to install more high-voltage cables above ground – and we need to get more capacity into the city as the population and the demand keep growing. So we have been boring underground – and will have completed the 32 kilometres we need by 2018.'

On a smaller scale, companies such as Western Power Distribution are responding to pressure from communities to put power lines underground. In the village of Edensor in the Peak District over 2 kilometres of cabling has been hidden. A similar project in the Malvern Hills Area of Outstanding Natural Beauty has resulted in the removal of lines from view. Construction work, though, can cause greater insult to the landscape than the pylons themselves, and after the cables have been sunk there are restrictions on what can and can't happen above them. Deep-rooted trees are actively discouraged, and industries like fracking would be problematic.

I had first come across fears about the impact of subterranean cabling in the early 1990s during the roll-out of cable TV, when Professor Chris Baines raised concerns that suburban trees would be killed as a result of their roots being sliced through. Fortunately, the media storm he kicked up resulted in contractors taking far greater care, and digging around the roots of big trees by hand.

When I phoned him to check on the story he was full of a new worry. 'We simply do not know enough about the way the roots of urban trees interact with our developed environment,' he began by saying – but then had to ring off as he was in the middle of making redcurrant jelly. This man of research, writing and consultancy was still living a life very much connected to the land about which he cares so deeply. 'There is a chronic loss of urban trees,' he subsequently went on, while his jelly was setting. 'The most dramatic I have seen was when the water main was replaced near where I live. Replacing the jointed metal pipe with a seamless plastic one has done the job and stopped the leaks. But this has also removed a source of water for the trees. And it got me wondering in particular about London and its amazing plane trees. There is a real need to repair leaking pipes, but we do not know what the consequences of this will be.'

He has a theory, though, and it is not one with a happy outcome. There are always new pathogens waiting to attack us and our wildlife, and one of the newest is Massaria, a fungal disease that was first recorded in plane trees in London in 2011, which causes branches to fall from infected trees. Chris is worried because he believes the fungus is triggered by drought. And with the plan to replace London's leaking water mains with a less porous linescape comes the removal of a valuable water source for the trees, creating drought and possibly creating a new calamity. The unintended consequences of such cryptic disturbances will continue to surprise us.

Above ground, meanwhile, the visual intrusion of the supporting pylons – the familiar lattice towers that began to bestride the country after a 1928 design competition won by the Milliken Brothers – is being addressed. I was shown a mock-up of the new design and it is certainly going to be

212

strikingly different: single T-topped poles with the cables hanging from the outstretched arms. I mentioned an image I had seen online of a large stag – with the cables running from the antlers. Ian suggested that this had probably been photoshopped.

Obviously I came to talk to the National Grid with some degree of prejudice. I do not like the look of pylons and cables in the landscape. They are a linescape I could, aesthetically at least, live without. Indeed, I find it strange how much fuss is made by the eternally conservative when confronted with the prospect of wind turbines or a solar farm, while the striding pylons are accepted as blending into the picturesque. With wind turbines I am not sure what is informing my aesthetic judgement – perhaps my political excitement at seeing energy supply being transformed overwhelms my worry as to their intrusion. But I still get a thrill from seeing turbines turn.

Ian Glover clearly believed there was far more to the Grid than just managing the negative. There was an ecological good from this linescape, he argued: one with much greater potential than just providing a convenient place for the pre-migration congregation of swallows. For out of the National Grid, Ian and his team have a mission to create the 'Natural Grid'.

There are nearly 250 substations around the country. Each of these has to be surrounded by a land buffer, free from development. And in the past these have largely been managed with neglect, resulting in pockets of valuable biodiversity. 'I am very much driven by the Lawton mantra, as I think all biodiversity managers should be,' Ian explained, 'of better, bigger and more connected.' The reference to Sir John Lawton's 2010 report, *Making Space for Nature*, was encouraging. Despite the great diversity of wildlife sites in England, Lawton concluded, these sites were 'too small and too isolated, leading to declines in many of England's characteristic species. With climate change, the situation is likely to get worse. This is bad news for wildlife but also bad news for us, because the damage to nature also means our natural environment is less able to provide the many services upon which we depend. We need more space for nature.'

So Ian Glover had got to thinking how best to create the change we need in his 250 pockets of semi-wild, and realised that they are, like all the best spiritual sites in the country, connected by straight lines. Only in this case there really are lines: the power lines that spread 7,000 kilometres across the country. Unfortunately he, or rather the Grid, does not own most of the land under these lines, but that does not mean there isn't the potential to start building a series of connections around the country.

Each landowner across whose land the pylons run already has to undertake certain management practices to ensure the efficient operation of the network; this includes not allowing trees to grow too tall beneath the power cables, for example. So there are already constructive relationships that can be cultivated. Working with the Wildlife Trusts, therefore, Ian has been developing these management plans to bring these linescapes to life. It takes time – there are a lot of people to talk to. He suggested I talk to the people at the Worcestershire

Wildlife Trust. The project between them and the National Grid had been running for three years now, and the results were beginning to take shape.

I arranged to meet the Trust's Caroline Corsie, and two members of the National Grid's landscape team, at a substation near the village of Astwood Bank. As she gave me directions over the phone, I tried to follow them on a map online. But I could see nothing on the road to Feckenham that looked like my destination, until I switched to satellite view. Here was a good reminder of how much maps can hide. This vast industrial site blossomed into view: 3 hectares of grey set into fields of green. Decked out in boots we headed off into the fields surrounding the substation to take stock of what had changed. Caroline, proof that being a grandparent need not slow you down, was clearly leading, so I fell into line with Cirhan Truswell and Chris Plester, both Sustainability Advisers to the Grid.

I had never inspected a substation very closely before. There was a menacing sense of barely contained energy. The rough pasture in the first field we entered had been used heavily for grazing in the preceding years. There was some hard standing, near the very secure fence shielding the fizz and crackle, which allowed cattle to loiter when the ground was excessively wet. The neglect had left the land scoured of most obvious signs of life. We can quickly change the land's character superficially, but unless we strip down the topsoil to bedrock, or slather the land in biocides, there is still going to be a residue, a memory of what once was, held in the soil.

As we talked I argued that if we developed the wildlife potential of linear features, especially hedgerows, we could worry less about ecologically ravaged fields like this. The edges could become both a refuge and a corridor for wildlife. Using linescapes such as power lines, I went on, we could even link up a re-wilded landscape with suburbia, allowing people to reconnect with wildlife.

Caroline was swift to deplore my lack of vision. She was not put off by a landscape like this at all. She was excited by the potential, and in particular the seed bank, the reservoir of seeds held in the soil that, given a chance, can re-bloom. 'You cannot ignore the quality of the soil that surrounds your lines if you are hoping they are going to provide the sort of network you dream of,' she said, and was happy to back her argument up with plenty of data. She put forward the attractive idea of 'safety corridors' to buffer the lines – so that the hedgerows, for example, would have strips of land dedicated to biodiversity running alongside them.

It was the buffer strip around the substation that particularly interested her. I conceived the land around the substation as a doughnut; she preferred to call it a halo of wilder growth. This is key to her plan to put the power lines to work for the benefit of nature. At the first point we stopped at in the halo there were obvious signs of work. Cattle, in particular longhorns, were in the field. The hedge that had become a gappy tree-line was being coerced back into hedge both by laying suitable remains and planting a mix of trees rich in fruit and flower like damson and dog rose. There was a fence to protect the re-growth and saplings – the cattle had inadvertently been undermining the efforts to assist the beautiful brown hairstreak, an often elusive butterfly which was known to be in the area, by eating the suckers and side shoots of the hedge on which the eggs were waiting to caterpillarise. A hedge was hardly revolutionary, but in this partnership with the National Grid Caroline had been encouraged to manage this tract of pasture to a degree that would never have been allowed if it had been a European-funded Stewardship Scheme, which offers farmers subsidies for carrying out environmentally beneficial measures.

The fence, I noticed, appeared to be upside-down: the larger holes in the wire were at ground level. Apparently it gets commented on every time the Wildlife Trust shows people this sort of fencing. But it is very deliberate. It is known as 'pheasant-friendly fencing' (being pheasant-friendly is not something I would encourage; they are a scourge, a weed) and has the distinct advantage of allowing non-flying creatures unfettered access.

Caroline was creating more than just a corridor; she was creating a vocabulary too. This power line was a 'fly-along', and along the way there were 'service stations'. The service stations are patches of land, like the area around the sub-station, that offer wildlife somewhere to recharge. They provide food, nectar, fruit and seeds, which in turn attract insects, as well as shelter – trees, bushes and even water. From where we stood, the powerlines loping up the slope ahead, I could see the potential. There were fifty-four towers to the next substation which, at 200 metres per tower, gives wildlife around 10 kilometres to the next service station. Caroline's service stations were temporal as well as physical. There was the obvious need to provide a feed along a journey, but also to help at those times of the year when scarcity hits. These were the 'hungry gaps' she looks to fill.

The newly reincarnated hedge led at right angles into an older hedge to form the edge of the halo. We turned left through a gate, and into another field of once over-grazed and over-nutrified grass that was now roughening up inside the 6-hectare halo. Spear and creeping thistle were battling it out with creeping and meadow buttercups. Forget-me-nots added a little delicacy, as did the blackfly aphids infesting the docks, soon to be food for swallows when the overcrowding on the leaves encouraged them to take flight.

'This field is being given a chance to express itself,' said Caroline, 'and it is not very pretty at the moment.' But the prettiness was breaking through. Meadow vetch with delicate pea-flowers was making some advance, and the patch of common bugle was a delight. I had not realised how like owls its flowers could look. Like the Great Fen, this was not a project for those with short attention spans. The Natural Grid would take time. Relationships would need to be nurtured as much as the soil.

The walk through the halo brought us to damper ground. Caroline presented me with two pieces of vegetation, telling me to run my fingers over them. One was smooth and round, the other triangular. 'Rushes are round and sedges have edges,' she said. I can imagine her grandchildren love her easy lessons.

Not all her lessons were as easy. She was a firm believer in the 'Natural Capital' model: the idea that if we can apportion a financial value to what nature provides it will be easier to argue for its protection – a view of life I've already said I find rather difficult. Deep down I feel we should appreciate nature for what she is, rather than require a price be put on what she does. But Caroline was persuasive. 'I am not interested in there being any trading of ecosystem services. I just want to be able to talk to the accounts team and the engineers about what I want to achieve in a language that they can understand.' A patch of ragged robin popped up near wild red clover. Caroline gave me a new word: 'ruderal'. It comes from the Latin for rubble, and refers to the plant species that are first to colonise disturbed land.

The management of the halo had convinced me, but the challenge was in allowing species to distribute radially from this service station. A lot of farmers who work land across which the power lines loop are instinctively suspicious of the potential burden they see coming with having to manage for wildlife. But Caroline's work is gaining respect. The increased biodiversity is being recognised, and the pragmatic way it is being achieved appreciated. For example, we know that hedge-laying is a wonderful way to create a diverse and rich corridor for wildlife, but also that it is expensive. So Caroline is looking at the less romantic, mechanised version, which involves a small digger pushing suitably sized trees down into a line – more like the behaviour of the large herbivores that once roamed this land than the delicate work with billhook and axe. Given that only 12 per cent of arable hedges are in good condition, the need to build the web of lines quickly is vital.

The farmers along Caroline's linescapes are not being faced

with a massively radical challenge. At the moment she is work-ing to persuade them to move towards 'conservation grazing' in the fields beneath the wires. Land is not taken out of pro-duction, just managed to improve the quality for wildlife. Both over- and under-grazing reduce the value of the habitat to wildlife, so management plans are produced to use the land optimally but still maintain or restore the ecological opportunities.

And there are more proactive schemes too. She has helped develop a 'Beneficial Insect Mix' of seeds to create extra stepping-stones along the lines. Planted around the base of the pylon, it is especially useful for intensive growers unable either to cultivate these patches themselves or free up produc-tive land for nature. The payback for the farmer is beneficial insects – both pollinators and pest predators.

The National Grid's linescapes traverse many different habitats. In woodland the need to prevent trees interfering with the cables has often resulted in dramatic and harsh edges, but now work is under way to soften them, and to reduce management costs by planting creatively. Specially selected varieties of fruit trees, therefore, are finding their way into linear orchards that will never grow up too close to the power lines, but will provide food and shelter for the wildlife using the fly-along.

No single habitat can flourish in isolation. But we have so fragmented the landscape with our lines that there are few areas living up to their potential. This vision of a Natural Grid I find really appealing. I believe it will become all the more necessary.

10

Unfragmentation

Unburn the boat, rebuild the bridge,
Reconsecrate the sacrilege . . .

'Recension Day', Duncan Forbes[1]

The linescape is everywhere, though sometimes less obvious.
To walk to a friend's house I can cut across a playing
field. Throughout the year the fringes of trees wax and
wane; the grass turns from churned mud to buttercup- and
daisy-sea. But the constant is the path – a desire path –
one that is made by the passage of feet rather than the
application of planning law. Each time I see this path I
smile. So like *A Line Made by Walking*, Richard Long's
famous photograph, but also so unlike it. Long walked a
path into the grass of a field, flattening out a line which he
then photographed. His line is straight: he walked back
and forth until his physical intervention was deep enough
to be recorded. My path is not straight – there is a meander,
a subtle sigmoid.

The cause is the shape of the gates. They guide us into
the field at an angle that requires correction to reach the far
side. And so is born an 'S' of different habitat. The line is

worn to mud, but alongside it there are parallel lines of darker grass, benefiting from the concentration of nutrients supplied by dogs on leads.

Wherever we leave our lines we are creating changes, some far more dramatic to our eyes than others. The brown corduroy of a freshly ploughed field might not seem a massive intrusion, but to some invertebrates the ridges will seem like a mountain range. And, of course, it can accelerate the loss of topsoil through erosion.

I remember a wonderful perspective shift that came from winning a ride in a hot-air balloon, and floating with some friends over the Lancashire countryside. The hedges below us were obvious, but what fascinated me was the way they had created other lines. A gate in the middle of a hedge was the wasp waist from which hoofprints fanned out. Deltas of bovine tracks.

Most of the lines I have investigated here are rather more intrusive. Across Europe new ones have started to appear. In an attempt to control the flow of people fleeing war and economic distress, barriers are being erected. In 2015, Slovenia began building a barbed-wire fence along its border with Croatia. By the time it had reached 140 kilometres it had already sliced through some of the richest wildlife habitat. And while the images of deer becoming entangled in wire managed to stir a reaction in the media, scientists are more worried about the impact this new line will have on smaller populations of carnivores, such as bears, lynx and wolves. Not only are some being killed by the wire as they try and scavenge, but their populations, already under pressure from humanity, are also becoming further fragmented.

These new barriers are exacting a horrible human toll as well, of course. But it could be the impact on wildlife that sees them being challenged through the international courts. The EU Habitats Directive requires open conservation corridors for the transboundary movement of animals. The opening of political borders towards the end of the last century has seen a great improvement in the populations of Europe's larger fauna. This is now under threat.

The threatened wall between Mexico and the USA, one of Donald Trump's more eccentric ideas, would have a devastating impact, not least on the slow recovery of the ocelot population. Wildlife does not understand the lines we draw on a map, only the barriers we erect along them.

Then again, there are walls being built which have an amazing potential. The 4,400-mile Great Green Wall, that will eventually stretch from Senegal to Djibouti, is being built to halt the advance of the Sahara Desert. No bricks-and-mortar; this will be a line of trees and other plants to hold back the encroaching erosion as well as providing food and medicine for the people living along it. Adopted by the African Union in 2007, 15 per cent complete in 2016, the Great Green Wall is a major international undertaking, a wall that will help millions and, when it is eventually completed, become the largest living structure on the planet, three times the size of the Great Barrier Reef.

Such examples show how important linescapes can be, and while we have not got anything quite on that scale happening in Britain, there are lines that we can use to make the 'Natural Grid' a reality. Sensitively done, lines can help break down barriers, allow wildlife to travel, and allow us the essential connection with a little bit of wild.

The modern-day enclosures created by road, rail and canal have done for wildlife what the eighteenth-century enclosures did for people. We have fragmented this country with a tracery of lines; we have created a linescape in the landscape. Wildlife within the pockets that remain needs a way to escape its enclosure.

Of course, there are solutions: reconnections can be made; we can re-consecrate the sacrilege. These reconnections can be more than just a mechanism for ecosystem-connectivity; they can be aesthetically very pleasing as well. In the Netherlands there are at the moment forty-seven wildlife bridges, also known as 'ecoducts', that have been built over linear infrastructure, proving that the dream of a planning process that takes wildlife seriously is not too far-fetched. The journey to this more enlightened state could be repeated here, if only there was the political will.

Hans Bekker worked for the national road authority in Holland for thirty-five years, during which time he witnessed the transition to a more ecological way of thinking. 'It started when we tried to improve our management of the verges of the main roads to benefit wild plants and insects, back in the early 1970s,' he explained to me. 'Then there was pressure to help our very small badger population – 20 per cent of which was killed on the roads each year. So we built the first badger tunnel in 1974. The next step was to build our first ecoduct, which we did in 1985, over an existing road.' In the 1990s it was decided that there should be no more fragmentation caused by new infrastructure. And if a new development did cause fragmentation, it had to have its impact reduced, or mitigated. If that was not possible, then there had to be compensation, and funds also had to be made available to repair past instances of fragmentation.

'This was stated in both the national infrastructure and national nature protection policies,' Hans explained. 'In 2004 parliament decided to instigate the Long-Term De-Fragmentation Programme. We had identified 215 points on the infrastructure network – the roads, railways and canals – where there were problems for wildlife, and have planned around 620 interventions, all the way from ecoducts and tunnels to extra fences. This was action at the national level, but there has also been work done on the regional and local scale too.' Of course these things are not free. The Dutch Ministry of Infrastructure pays the bill for both de-fragmentation of existing roads and new-build.

In *Green Bridges, A Literature Review*, a report published by Natural England in 2015, the absence of interest in nature connectivity in this country is marked. The very few examples it could find from Britain contrast dramatically with the real work that has gone on in the continent. In some countries, the report conceded, it almost goes without saying that 'crossings will be constructed for fauna when new road and railway infrastructure is built'.[2]

For these living bridges to work, as we can see from countries like the Netherlands, they need to be wide. Deer, for example, hardly used ecoducts that were 5 metres wide, but when they were 50 metres wide, not only were they used by a whole host of wildlife, but they also became habitats themselves. Using sand traps to record footprints, researchers found that deer (red, roe and fallow), boar, fox, badger, mice, shrews and voles all used a 50-metre-wide overpass at Terlet. Another ecoduct in the Netherlands, at Groene Woud, was specifically designed with reptiles and amphibians in mind. A motorway was being built through a wetland area, so now there is a 50-metre-wide habitat complete with small pools fed from stored rainwater that is pumped up when needed.

The most important thing about such projects, however, is that they are not a fantasy. Whether by landscape bridges, canopy crossings, or underpasses of various designs, we can help wildlife reconnect with the habitat it needs to be able to thrive. In the USA, indeed, there is a move to remove roads altogether – completely erase them from the landscape. Both the Forest Service and the National Parks have begun to mitigate the impact on wildlife in this permanent and dramatic way. In the northern Rocky Mountains, for example, researchers have found that where roads have been removed the ability of wildlife, in particular black bears, to hunt further afield has been accompanied by a reduction in human interference and poaching.

The few examples we have from Britain tend to be rather more timid – tunnels being provided for wildlife, rather than bridges. More than sixty were built under the Northern Relief Road around Birmingham – not because there was empirical evidence of their efficacy, but simply because they seemed like a good idea. Research done by the conservation charity Froglife, however, has shown how some wildlife will enter tunnels, but not make the complete journey, because the temperature drops further in. This is particularly true for amphibians and reptiles. A further point raised by Froglife's Conservation Co-ordinator, Silviu Petrovan, is the distinction between use and effectiveness. Just because bats are seen to use a structure does not mean it is effective as a conservation tool. We need to look beyond individual animals to the population as a whole.

Silviu's work has also highlighted the need for any interventions to be well maintained. Fences must guide species to underpasses, and if they are to do their job they must remain intact. Too much emphasis is put on contractors merely completing a job, and not enough on managing it over time. Other problems arise when species try to share the same space. We know that badger activity will prevent hedgehogs moving along hedge-lines, so it's not difficult to imagine their presence will impede hedgehogs' use of underpasses.

With other countries proving that we can create functional interventions it needs a simple shift in priorities to enable the same thing to happen in Britain. So what can be done? A frequent retort is the punchline from the old joke: 'I wouldn't start from here.' Lars Nilson, the Environment Director of the Swedish Transport Administration, perhaps puts it better: 'An infrastructure in harmony with the landscape is easy and cheap if done right from the beginning.'

That is not where we are, so we need to conjure a persuasive argument that will work on many levels – appeal to the head and the heart. We need to convince gardeners to make holes in fences for hedgehogs, councils to rein in their mowing regime to allow flowers to flourish, and infrastructure projects to put ecology on a level with economy.

All of our lines, as we have seen, have the potential to help wildlife. Even the least promising, litter-strewn, death-delivering, habitat-fragmenting linescapes could provide a link, a line of connectivity. Danish scurvy grass has made our main roads its home. The Grand Union Canal that passes by Edward Chell's studio is the same body of water that otters use to get under the M42 100 miles to the north.

How much more could be achieved if these links were deliberate? If we were to view the ecosystem on a landscape-wide scale? Running green and blue lines into cities, for example, would benefit people as well as wildlife.

It is not as if this dream is undreamt. Professor Sir John Lawton, whose writing kicked off this journey for me, set out a vision that should have equal status with any aspirations for health and education. In *Making Space for Nature* he recognised the conspicuous absence of habitat fragmentation from the conservation conversation, and suggested a remedy. Five components to connectivity: core areas of high nature-conservation value, corridors and stepping-stones, restoration areas, buffer zones, and sustainable-use areas.

This would cost, of course. His dream came with a price tag of £1.1 billion a year for nature conservation. That would go some way to making the change. But before you balk at such a figure, I'd argue that we need to start taking threats to biodiversity as seriously as we take threats from terrorism and banks. As a society, we can find billions to address problems like these. But without a viable ecosystem we are presented with an existential crisis that makes money and bombs pale into insignificance.

So before writing off the call for £1.1 billion a year, consider that the estimated cost of renewing the Trident nuclear missile system is around £205 billion. Since 2007 the UK Treasury has committed to spending £1.162 trillion on bailing out the banks. We could meet Lawton's demands for two centuries if we repurposed the money spent on Trident – or for a millennium, if we had not been propping up the banks. And what would present the best return for society? There is enough money for nature's need, not our greed, to misquote Gandhi. I decided to ask Professor Sir John Lawton himself how he felt his vision had been implemented.

Now retired, Sir John is one of those people who seems to be as busy as ever. He was generous, open and delightfully unguarded. The part of his report that moved me most was its optimism – that he really believed a change was possible. Given the perspective of time, had this view faded?

'Outside of government there is a heck of a lot going on,' he told me. 'People "get it" – they understand the need to develop corridors for wildlife. But this present government is an utter disaster. They have torn up ten major environmental initiatives such as green houses and car emissions, in the face of their manifesto commitments. The derogation for neo-nicotinoids [the UK giving farmers permission to use these bee-killing chemicals despite an EU ban] flies in the face of the evidence. Outside government there are some really encouraging activities; within, there is a complete lack of comprehension as to what it means to leave the environment in a better shape.'

So what was the single most important thing necessary to arrest the decline in biodiversity and bioabundance in the UK by 2030?

'There are two key things,' replied Sir John swiftly. 'We need to properly recognise the economic benefits of the environment – carbon storage, flood prevention, health benefits. And we need to heavily tax any environmentally damaging activity. How much is a skylark worth? Clearly it is not nothing, and it is not an infinite figure, so it is some-where between. The work that nature does has value and we can quantify this.'

My heart began to sink. Here was someone I respect advo-cating, in part, something that just felt instinctively wrong. Yes, I understand how he gets to the point where a skylark has a value, but I disagree with the value placed on the process itself. If we start to think of wildlife in pecuniary terms, I worry, we will stop caring for it with those less-quantifiable markers of love and respect.

Some time after our conversation, as is always the case when desperately reaching for a retort, I had a moment of enlightenment. There is a famous atheist saying: 'Just be good for goodness' sake.' To call on people to act with kindness, motivated not by fear of a vengeful and insecure deity, but because it is the good thing to do, strikes me as entirely reasonable. And now I look on people's need to give nature a value in order to protect it in much the same light. Is it absurdly naïve to think we might put a value on nature because it is priceless?

But Sir John Lawton is still locked into the monetary mind-set, and it is frustratingly persuasive. I just worry where it will lead. 'It is strange that humans value things made by humans far more than those made by the natural world,' he reflected. 'I feel it is simply wrong to put a greater value on, say, a museum full of treasures than an ancient woodland.'

Asking for £1.1 billion a year and receiving just £7.5 million would suggest the worth of Sir John's work was far from being recognised. Was he disappointed?

'I am not disappointed with the money. I argued that we needed £1.1 billion for national nature conservation. What we got was always going to be seed corn – it started the twelve Nature Improvement Areas and levered about £4.50 for every pound given in the first place. Of course, it would have been nice to have had more. The most disappointing part of the money was that when the coalition government fell the new lot cut central funding to the NIAs, despite the government trumpeting them as a success story.' Sir John suggested I look at one of the programmes that began life as an NIA, and is now the Humberhead Levels Living Landscape project in Yorkshire.

This 2,000-square kilometre site at the western end of the Humber estuary is a flat plain occupying the site of the glacial Lake Humber that was created by water being dammed by the glacial moraine. Now it straddles the borders of Lincolnshire, Nottinghamshire and Yorkshire, and is rich in wildlife and human activity. Farming mingles with rivers, dykes with a mosaic of wetlands. It is managed in a partnership of twelve organisations, and is living proof of seeing large to save small. Conservation efforts were being directed at encouraging the Thorne pin-palp beetle, the bog hog beetle, the hairy canary fly and the scarce vapour moth as much as the bittern, all threatened in the face of an impending change in climate. Important though the management of the watery linescape of rivers, ditches and drains has been, enhancing connectivity between the wetland areas has been as much about making connections with the farming community as muddy work in waders. So far they have delivered 1,190 hectares of better, bigger, more joined-up wildlife habitat – clearly taking inspiration from Lawton's proposition.

The first iteration of Nature Improvement Areas, though, had serious shortcomings. 'There was a lack of leadership,' Tim Graham, the manager of the project, explained when I spoke to him. 'We tried to share information, but it took until the closing months of the funding for all twelve projects to meet. Then the funding dried up, and now we are back to maintaining our own patches.' How fascinating that one of the stumbling blocks was the structural fragmentation between the different groups!

Another Yorkshire project that excited John Lawton was in the Yorkshire Dales National Park, on restoring hay meadows in Swaledale. These are not linear features on their own, of course, but a series of them acts as stepping-stones, a sort of cryptic linear feature. In Wiltshire, meanwhile, another NIA is doing great work on the Marlborough Downs, and in this case has been taken on by the local farmers, a bottom-up approach to conservation that is showing great potential. A key aim, in the 10,000 hectares brought into the project, is to re-establish the tree sparrow. That might sound quite a timid aspiration, but this is a bird that between 1970 and 2008 saw its population collapse by 93 per cent. And as with most ecological projects, what helps one species often helps a whole raft of others.

My memories of the Marlborough Downs are a little bleak. My boarding school had an annual cross-country run that I recall as never less than desolate and painful, the bleakness of the ordeal compounded by the barren surroundings: the prairies of the crop-baron with rooks waiting to peck our still-warm flesh when we fell. Now, however, life is returning to fields that have felt the hand of man since at least the Neolithic period.

Tree sparrows need water. Chalk downs are notoriously dry, the water draining swiftly through the porous rock. Dew ponds, though, were once a staple of this sort of land: shallow ponds, lined with clay that collected rain water and stored it for livestock. Now a series of sixteen new dew ponds have been created, relying not on clay this time but pond liners. They are described by one of the project's co-ordinators as a 'necklace' – a linear feature made up of watery jewels, strung out along the Downs to provide the kind of 'service stations' described by Caroline Corsie in the previous chapter.

The dew ponds provide more than just water; they help provide the insects the tree sparrows need for their young. Within six months of their being dug, dragonflies have emerged, and even fish, which must have arrived in the beaks or on the feet of ducks. Around the ponds nectar-rich plants are favoured and seed plants that are not harvested, creating a series of bird tables across what was hostile ground. Now, 86 per cent of the NIA is within a mile of a reliable water source. This virtual linescape has also provided scrub cover as shelter from predators, and nest boxes have been put up. The result has been that tree sparrows have increased in number and begun to spread. But perhaps the greatest connections have been among the community of people who live and work on the Downs. Farmers and conservationists working together have managed to open up and connect far more land than they could have done on their own.

Working with just forty-two farms made the Marlborough Downs project achievable: the number of stakeholders was manageable. Which made me wonder how an NIA-inspired offshoot, the Hedgehog Improvement Area of Solihull, was going to cope.

Run by the Warwickshire Wildlife Trust – similar initiatives are emerging in Stockport, Chester, Oxford and Ipswich – this project has employed someone to do a job perhaps I should have applied for: a Hedgehog Officer, to work on countering the physical and the social barriers to a hedgehog-friendly environment. 'We found that gardens are becoming more isolated,' Simon Thompson explained when I went to meet him. 'People are becoming more insular, and when an old fence or hedge needs replacing they are going for what they perceive as increased security, with bigger fences. And once one person does that, others follow. There is much less communication over the fence and, at the same time, much less communication under the fence too. We have to move away from "armchair conservation"', he went on, 'and recognise that if we are to make a difference we need the active engagement of people. They need to know it is not superheroes in capes who change the world.'

So the mission was to get into the fortified suburbs and break through these linear features, these fences. 'We are doing it the old-fashioned way,' Simon said. 'We're knocking on doors and going into schools. Not completely cold-calling – we are leafleting first – but this is really basic work, reaching out to the community, asking them to think about hedgehogs. We are looking for volunteers to have tracking tunnels in their gardens to get an idea of how many actually have hedgehogs, then we see whether this number increases after we have encouraged and facilitated changes.'

The tracking tunnels have generated plenty of data, which is a double win for Simon. 'Not only are we seeing where the hedgehogs are, and which gardens they prefer, but we are also able to show the participants some proper ecological work in action. It is easy to underestimate how important the excitement and the engagement of the public is for this sort of work.'

The hope is that the HIA in Solihull will build on the work we at the British Hedgehog Preservation Society and the People's Trust for Endangered Species started in 2011 with the Hedgehog Street campaign, when we encouraged people to make their gardens wildlife-friendly and put a small hole in the fence to allow hedgehogs to move between gardens. Then, having shown it is possible to improve the lot of the hedgehog on a larger scale, you can roll out the project to other areas. Maybe one day developers will build and then market new houses as 'hedgehog-friendly'.

*

But what of the national infrastructure? In fact, something almost as substantial as the Great Green Wall of Africa is looming. Britain's largest infrastructure project of modern times, HS2, could just be business as usual. But perhaps those tasked with driving the new high-speed railway from London to Birmingham and onward will be brave. What my exploration of Britain's linescapes has proved is that bad lines can be redeemed. Better still, new lines can be crafted with best practice to become an infrastructure of which we can be proud. Because this 330-mile slice through the country has the potential to become a really valuable nature-restoration project.

The current plans for HS2 would see thousands of hectares of important wildlife habitat lost and many more fragmented. Four of the government-originated Nature Improvement Areas will be affected, and promises of offsetting can never replace the thirty-four ancient woodland sites that would be destroyed. But what if a radical approach was to be taken and this narrow linescape was to be enlarged? How about a kilometre-wide ribbon of wildlife-rich habitat patches on either side? It may sound fantastical, but it is not. The Wildlife Trusts have floated this innovative alternative.

The new living line would provide an opportunity for existing wildlife sites to be connected and improved, either by allowing natural regeneration or by recreating good habitat along its length. A 'Low-Speed 2' network of foot, cycle and bridle paths would help connect people to wildlife sites along its length. Communities of both wildlife and people fragmented by the necessary 80-metre-wide dead zone of railway would be linked by landscape bridges integrated into appropriate habitat. The land would be managed by a partnership of residents, landowners and experts for the benefit of both people and wildlife. All it would take is a little bravery – and a clear statement as to the importance of nature.

The cost, even if we leave out the dubious accounting of natural capital, would not be extortionate. To reconnect or renew 15,000 hectares and create 120 miles of new cycle and foot paths would require £130 million, with an additional £10 million per year for maintenance and rent. Which is, and this is the clincher, less than 1 per cent of the HS2 budget. And as the Wildlife Trusts remind us, we should be ensuring that those who govern us live up to their promises.

'Whether we live in the city or the countryside,' wrote the former Secretary of State for Environment, Food and Rural Affairs Caroline Spelman in the *Natural Choice* white paper of 2011, 'natural systems support us. The natural environment becomes degraded when people lose their sense of contact with it. Human health and happiness also suffer. This White Paper aims to strengthen connections between people and nature, to the benefit of both.' The White Paper went on to say that 'The Government wants this to be the first generation to leave the natural environment of England in a better state than it inherited.'[3]

The truth that underpins those statements has not changed, but the emphasis on nurturing nature has since all but vanished from government. In 2015, for example, came the Deregulation Act, a meta-regulation that requires all regulators to now 'have regard to the desirability of promoting economic growth'. Unless the natural capital accountants become far more robust this is going to be a constant obstacle to efforts to protect the natural world. It is not as if money invested in nature would vanish. Given some intelligent accounting, expenditure on conservation is quickly recouped.

The inspirational academic Jules Pretty has argued that we should accommodate the management of nature inside the Department of Health, such is its contribution to the population's wellbeing. The positive impact of time spent close to nature on children who need help with concentration is far greater than prescriptions of Ritalin. Or perhaps the Department of Education should get in on the act. A recent report from Natural England, *Natural Connections*, proved how effective the outdoors was at improving the attainment of children, especially those from deprived areas. Hopefully learning amid the natural environment will become a recognised method of improving not only academic marks, but also children's health and wellbeing. At Cambridge University, indeed, Laurie Parma has been collecting evidence for the health benefits of nature during her study of neuro-psychopharmacology, and has developed an app called NatureBuzz, which gathers evidence of where and when you are feeling good or bad to see how this correlates with your surroundings.

Oscar Wilde was warning about the cynic when he wrote of people who 'know the price of everything and the value of nothing'. But he went on, 'And a sentimentalist ... is a man who sees an absurd value in everything, and doesn't know the market place of any single thing.' Perhaps I am a bit of a sentimentalist when it comes to the natural world, but I have no shame in thinking that there are intrinsic values that cannot be priced. 'Scientists do themselves a disservice,' Andrew Lack, a botanist at Oxford Brookes University, said to me, 'if they ignore the importance of the unquantifiable.' He was talking about that tricky subject, love. Love is truly priceless. A more forthright critique comes from the philosopher Murray Bookchin:

> The moral pieties that are voiced by many well-meaning environmentalists are as naïve as the moral pieties of multinationals are manipulative. Capitalism can no more be 'persuaded' to limit growth than a human being can be 'persuaded' to stop breathing. Attempts to 'green' capitalism, to make it 'ecological,' are doomed by the very nature of the system as a system of endless growth.[4]

Throughout this journey I have been repeatedly confronted with the 'natural capital' argument. Nature is expected to pay, and if it can't pay, it can't stay, and will have to make way for 'progress'. So many people working in the real world of organisms, rather than the remote world of spreadsheets, are being won over, but with evident distaste. One senior conservationist talked of feeding at the same table as accountants, but with the very longest of spoons.

We just need to find a way to present biophilia in a politically agreeable manner – to remind those with power that we all have an intrinsic need for connection with the natural world. How deeply seated this need is has been explored in MRI studies of the brain activity of volunteers shown images of different environments. Urban views excite and agitate; wild views calm and relax. How, then, can we build ecological sensitivity into the design and maintenance of an effective infrastructure? Relying on governments is clearly never going to be enough.

In the summer of 2016 I was invited to the first large workshop organised by the Linear Infrastructure Network. LINet has, for the first time, brought together groups such as Network Rail, Highways England, the Canal and River Trust, the National Grid, the Wildlife Trusts, the RSPB, academics, developers, government agencies and ecological consultants, with the express purpose of improving the linear features that connect and fragment us and the natural world. Over seventy organisations are collaborating in this informal network, and as the doers meet the thinkers, and both try and influence the policymakers, there is a real sense of optimism.

This is extremely exciting. The ideas that were brewing as I started writing this book have already started to take practical shape. I wish I could claim credit for it, but in reality it is more evidence of an idea that is coming into its own. Connectivity is key to conservation.

LINet has been pulling together case studies showing good practice, and is producing a guide that 'seeks to optimise the potential of linear infrastructure to address and enhance ecological fragmentation and secure greater connectivity nationally, regionally and locally'. A key challenge is to get good practice accepted as 'business as usual'. There are nearly 400,000 hectares of road and rail soft estate alone, ripe with potential. LINet organiser Nicholas White, from Natural England, described how they alone, if managed well, could more than double the Government's target for habitat creation. 'And even more significantly, this estate can enhance ecological connectivity across rural and urban landscapes, delivering benefits for people and wildlife alike.'

Weaving in the old with the new is key – using the linear features already present to assist in making the grey lines green. But this is not a gathering of dreamers; this is underpinned by research. The political landscape requires everything to pay, so this is not going to be about scattering wildlife bridges and calling it a success. We need research to uncover nature's wish list, and then we need to measure that against the demands of development. Better to learn what destruction we, as a society and an ecosystem, can live with, than for those less sensitive to nature's needs to be given a free hand. Then find a mechanism that generates compensation commensurate with the real cost.

At last it feels that the linescape we have etched into this country is being taken seriously. There is even talk of a real effort being made to join up all of our National Parks, creating wildlife corridors to make this dream a reality. We might not be about to get a Minister for Lines, but we can and should value the work of the Linear Infrastructure Network.

Here are the people who can take the theories and aspirations of dreamers like me and turn them into reality. My wildlife dreams are born of years outdoors, trailing hedgehogs along hedgerows or just relishing the contact with nature in garden, park or further afield. Contact with nature is crucial to my well-being. And of course I am not alone; it is innate to us all. We need nature – and nature needs us to need it, so we will do what we can to ensure it thrives.

Nicholas White knew about my research, and in particular my quest to find examples of reconnection in the landscape. He asked if I had ever been to the Devil's Punchbowl in Surrey. When I said no, he gave me a simple injunction. Go.

11

Reconnection

Looking down on the A3 as it thundered beneath my feet, I felt a strange sense of calm. Despite the tarmac gash there was a sense of connection, even of wellbeing, as I leaned over the concrete wall. New roads can deliver an ecological good.

I was standing on Miss James's Bridge, built to remember the local resident who had been a generous supporter of the fledgling National Trust, which was nowadays the custodian of the magnificent natural phenomenon nearby that is the Devil's Punchbowl. The floor of the bridge was carpeted with rabbit-cropped grass and planted with heather and other heathland flora, ensuring continuity of habitat between Nutcombe and Tyndall's Wood, which it connected, for reptiles and amphibians, as well as a functioning bridleway.

This reconnection was but one small component of the wider transformation that has come over this Surrey landscape. Ahead of me were two dark holes, like eyes in the hillside, one swallowing, the other ejecting a steady stream of traffic: 30,000 vehicles a day, that once cut the Devil's Punchbowl in two. Half an hour earlier I had been part of that stream as I drove through this, at 1,830 metres the longest tunnel under dry land in Britain.

For decades there had been a fight over how to increase the capacity of this section of the A3. For most of its 100 kilometres between London and Portsmouth it was dual-carriageway, but just down the road at Hindhead there was a bottleneck as it was reduced to just three lanes. The obvious option, to copy the M3 at Twyford Down or the Newbury Bypass, was to blast a wider corridor, laying waste the wildlife along the way. But doggedly determined opposition from the residents eventually won out. Rather than increasing the fragmentation of the landscape with a vicious cut, the decision was taken to bore a tunnel.

As I headed back up to where I had left my car at the National Trust tea room, I noticed a path to my right, traversed about 6 metres up by a wire tunnel – a dormouse bridge. More reconnections. The path took me through a moisty woodland of old trees: oak and hazel, rhododendron and rowan, its floor carpeted with the first fall of leaves. The early-autumn rot was charging the air with change: bracket fungi dusted trunks with cinnamon-coloured spores; a flock of tits piped above. One of the flickers of movement was not quite tit-like, so I stopped and waited. Bold and small, a goldcrest was skipping under beech leaves, gleaning minute prey. However, the calm was not complete: it was impossible to lose the roar of traffic; like a sea that never breaks, the monotonous surge of rubber on tarmac permeated everything. It was not until I got to the edge of the Punchbowl that the drone vanished.

Standing at the lookout I was gazing across the 600 metres or so to the other side when an elderly couple joined me, and we started to talk. They pointed out on the far side of the bowl what I had taken to be a path. 'That was the A3,' the man said.

'Oh, you remember that day,' said his wife, 'when they closed the road? And we got to walk along it, and hear the birds singing and breathe fresh air? Wasn't it special!'

It had taken forty years to achieve this unfragmentation – forty years of planning meetings, debate, decisions made and unmade. The financial cost was considerable, at £155,000 for every metre of tunnel. And even when the tunnel had opened there had been a campaign among some in the community to keep the old A3 open . . . just in case. A fair extension of that logic would be to tarmac everywhere, just in case.

The Bowl, a wonderful natural amphitheatre fringed by mature trees, is a sloping heath that gives way to denser vegetation at the bottom. We talked about the name given to this SSSI. It was easy to see where the mythology came from. Did two giants fight here? And when one scooped up the earth to hurl at the other, missing them, did that create both the Bowl and the Isle of Wight? Or was it the imprint of the Devil's backside after he leapt from the Devil's Dyke near Brighton? Possibly it is the result of springs that gradually hollowed out a cavern, which then collapsed.

Following the couple's directions I headed off to find the old road. Walking among oaks I was struck again by the peace, broken only by the excitable barks of dogs as they bounced about. I came upon a faint clearing, which provided an arena for the fluid fisticuffs of robins singing their fight, staking their claim; and, above and around them, long-tailed tits, playing. Before me, a path: grass-covered; older trees dropping away to the left, bracken leading into heather; rowan and younger trees rising up to my right.

Without realising, I had already started to walk along the former route of the A3. For 200 years where I was standing had been the highway linking London and Portsmouth. Now it was a byway, being returned to what it once was: a green lane. The heath that had been sliced through by three lanes of traffic and many thousands of vehicles a day, the peace that had been shattered by the noise and fumes, the connections that had been severed by tarmac, truck and car – all now unfragmented, re-joined in joyful life. And joy is what I felt, walking where I would have been mown down, grinning at the birds. I felt like skipping.

I carried on around the edge of the Punchbowl. To one side of me house martins played with the air in the hollow; to the other another flock of long-tailed tits joyfully frolicked in the wooded ridge. I know they were all feeding, ripping through the last of the autumn's invertebrates, but they were all doing it with such apparent glee. The ridge had once hid highwaymen; now it was mainly labradors and spaniels that leapt from the bracken and heather.

I climbed up from the A3 to a gap in the trees on the higher ridge, and the Ordnance Survey trig point for Gibbet Hill; some of the highwaymen swung here for months. At 282 metres above sea level, even on this hazy day, you could still make out Canary Wharf some 60 kilometres away to the north-east.

This is a safe and good wild, I thought. We forget that we are animals too; we need wildness in our everyday lives.

We need natural complexity, diversity and abundance, not simplified monocultures – why else do grey squirrels get so much attention in London parks? We flourish in contact with wildlife. But it is more than just the connection with an animal: it is to do with our need to experience, however removed or dilute, the thrill of loss of control. Maintaining the veneer of civility is tough. It was not that long ago we were as wild as the animals we now venerate on television.

So how can we pull a little more wildness into our lives? Well, I believe this is where our linescapes have such a role to play. Clearly a self-willed landscape is incompatible with suburbia, which relies so completely on our will being imposed on the landscape. But for our gardens to have the flourish that will thrill, there needs to be a connection to the source, to a wilder world. The Devil's Punchbowl is hardly the great wilderness, but it is a source of *wildness*, and by establishing such a daring reconnection, this wildness can begin to flow.

The current design of cities is to constrain them within a belt, a belt of green. The idea is great: halt sprawl, stop cities merging into one grey block, and provide a little breathing-space within easy reach of their populations. But the green is itself often quite grey – horsieculture or intensive agriculture, not the hotbeds of biodiversity we need to feed the souls of our cities. To get the green into town there needs to be a link, a connection from wilder lands beyond. And that is where our linescapes can bridge the gap.

At the heart of my desire for an unfragmented landscape is an unashamedly romantic yearning for something I have only glimpsed. I am too young to have experienced the beauty Britain had to offer. I was born after the war had begun: the war against the land, mechanisation that erupted as the screaming brat of the first incarnation of industrial revolution – swarming out of the factories and into the fields with an iron fist.

I know I am not alone in craving more. The popularity of wildlife programmes and membership of conservation organisations confirms that millions see nature as a good thing. But our challenge is to turn this 'good' into 'essential' – so that those millions see the protection of the natural world as something as vital as feeding our children.

That gap between good and essential is a fragmentation as real as any faced by wildlife in our linear landscape. We are cut off from nature – a schism only emphasised by the brilliance with which wildlife is depicted on television. We feel we have 'done' nature from the comfort of our own sofa. Those of us moved to act feel we have achieved something by clicking on a box on a social media website. We risk being lulled by liking.

We must get off the sofa, and explore the connections that already exist. Visit a Dartmoor reave. Seek out the green lanes; use your feet to keep them open. Brave a canal; walk out into the countryside alongside these blue lanes that feed the city. Try not to shy away from the power lines, but look at them as a potential route through the countryside. Lay a hedge. Search for the money-safe stones out there in the walls. See beyond the line of litter on the verge and recognise the potential of this soft estate. And finally, look out of the train window. Our linescapes follow us; it is up to us not to let them govern us. It is time to take these lines back for good.

NOTES

Introduction

1 Roman Krznaric, *pers. comm.*, 22.11.16

1. Archaeological Lines

1 The Sweet is not a reference to the very pleasing nature of such lines, but to Mr Ray Sweet, who found the first evidence of it.

2 M. J. Allen, B. Chan, R. Cleal, C. French, P. Marshall, J. Pollard, R. Pullen, C. Richards, C. Ruggles, D. Robinson, J. Rylatt, J. Thomas, K. Welham and M. Parker Pearson, 'Stonehenge's Avenue and "Bluestonehenge"', *Antiquity*, 90(352), 2016, pp. 991–1008.

3 The most detailed analysis comes in Andrew Fleming's *The Reaves of Dartmoor* (London, Batsford, 1988).

2. Hedges

1 E. Pollard, M. D. Hooper and N. W. Moore, *Hedges* (New Naturalist no. 58, London, William Collins, 1974), p. 21.

2 Oliver Rackham, *The History of the Countryside* (London, Weidenfeld & Nicolson, 1995), p. 185.

3 Jules Pretty, *Agri-Culture, Reconnecting People, Land and Nature* (London, Earthscan, 2002).

4 E. P. Thompson, *The Making of the English Working Class*, (London, Penguin, 2013).

5 John Clare, 'The Mores' (London, Penguin, 1990), pp. 169–171.

6 Edward Thomas, *One Green Field* (London, Penguin, 2009), p. 42.

7 George Monbiot, *Guardian*, 28 May 2013.

8 Georg Muller, *Europe's Field Boundaries*, (Stuttgart, Neuer Kunstverlag, 2014)

9 *Between Fences* (Princeton, National Building Museum & Princeton Architectural Press, 1996), p. 65.

10 Rackham, *op. cit.,* p. 182.

11 Muller, *op. cit.*

12 (editors) David W. Macdonald and Ruth E. Feber, *Wildlife Conservation on Farmland. Managing for Nature on Lowland Farms* (Oxford, Oxford University Press, 2015), pp. 20–42.

13 George Monbiot, 'The Pricing of Everything', *Guardian*, 24 July 2014.

14 'Life in a hedge', *British Wildlife*, June 2015.

15 Rackham, *op. cit.,* pp. 194–202

16 'Life in a hedge', *op. cit.*

4. Walls

1 https://markcocker.wordpress.com/2014/07/22/north-ronaldsay-an-island-in-two-seas/

2 K. C. Edwards, H. H. Swinnerton and R. H. Hall, *The Peak District* (New Naturalist no. 44, London, William Collins, 1962), p. 176.
3 Oliver Rackham, *op. cit.*
4 *The Peak District, op. cit.,* p. 63.
5 *Wildlife Conservation on Farmland, op. cit.,* p. 45.

5. Ancient Paths and Green Lanes
1 *Edward Thomas,* (London, Faber, 2016), p. 157.

6. Canals
1 L. T. C. Rolt, *Navigable Waterways* (London, Arrow, 1973).
2 ibid.
3 ibid.
4 Roy Martin, 'The Chemical Traffic – A legacy from the past' (2013), http://www.whatliesbeneathrattlechainlagoon.org.uk
5 'Invasive Species in Europe: ecology, status and update', *Environmental Sciences Europe*, June 2011.

7. Railways
1 http://www.railway-technical.com/statistics.shtml
2 C. N. Trueman, http://www.historylearningsite.co.uk
3 http://www.networkrail.co.uk/timetables-and-travel/delays-explained/leaves/
4 S. A. Harris, 'Introduction of Oxford Ragwort, *Senecio squalidus* L. (Asteraceae), to the United Kingdom', *Watsonia* 24, 2002, pp. 31–43.

5 https://www.gov.uk/government/collections/biodiversity-offsetting

8. Roads
1 *Safe Passages: Highways, Wildlife, and Habitat Connectivity* (Washington DC, Island Press, 2010).

10. Unfragmentation
1 'Recension Day', reproduced with kind permission of the author, Duncan Forbes.
2 http://publications.naturalengland.org.uk/publication/6312886965108736
3 https://www.gov.uk/government/publications/the-natural-choice-securing-the-value-of-nature
4 Murray Bookchin, *Remaking Society*, (Black Rose, 1998).

ACKNOWLEDGEMENTS

The idea for this book had been brewing for years, but it took the faith of my agent, James Macdonald Lockhart, to help make it a reality. Rob MacFarlane encouraged me generously. Rosemary Davidson from Square Peg caught the idea and, with the help of Graham Coster, has made *Linescapes* something of which I am very proud.

The book would not have been possible without the many advocates of lines I met along the way: Olaf Bayer, Simon Blackbourn, Trevor Wragg, Valerie Belsey, Jo Bell, Mark Robinson, Helen Bailey, Mark Ullyett, Rob Dingle, Octavia Neeves, Edward Chell, David Lovejoy, Tony Sangwine, Ian Glover, Caroline Corsie, Silviu Petrovan, Nicholas White, the Hedgehog Street team and many others who have inadvertently joined me on this journey.

The name, Linescapes, came from a wine-fuelled evening with Robin Bennett when I was at the end of my tether trying to capture the idea in a word. Thank you for that – and Wood Festival, and letting me indulge my passions with my Kindling stage each year.

The process of writing a book can seem isolated, but I have been fortunate to have a gang of fellow writers and thinkers to moan to and with, as we manage the small orchard we share: Kate Raworth, Roman Krznaric, Casper Henderson, George Monbiot, Rebecca Wrigley and Cristina Mateos Arribas.

The New Networks for Nature has been a constant source of inspiration.

Beds, love and support have come from Anne and Edward Gleave, Ishka Michocka, Emily Miles, Debbie Lomas, Stephen Hancock, Chloe and Christian de Sousa, George Marshall, Annie Levy, Jenny Broughton, Miriam Darlington, Lucy Durneen, Amy Grace-Fensome, Jay Griffiths, Gordon Maclellan, Lisbet and Oliver Tickell, David Broughton, Theo Simon, Shannon Smy, Eylan and Leisle Ezekiel, Dominic Woodfield, Huma Pearce and my dancing tribe.

'Odd-daughters' Naia and Rosa – I look forward to being a bad influence on you as you all get taller than me. Silva, continue to shine.

Lastly, my family, tolerant as ever; I hope that Mati and Pip enjoy seeing their names in print, and that Zoe and my mother are proud of what they have helped create.

INDEX

A
Agutter, Jenny 154
Aickman, Robert 130
ancient paths 102–7, 116
   see also green lanes
Anthropocene period 6
Ashby canal, Leicestershire 146
assarts 46
Australia 178

B
badgers 39–40, 57, 76–7, 89,
   119, 141, 152, 157, 161, 163,
   178, 224, 226–7
Bailey, Helen 62–72
Baines, Chris 211–12
Bamburgh, Northumbria 30
bank voles 5
barbed wire 45–6
bats 56, 94, 139, 142–3, 145,
   165–7, 200
Bayer, Olaf 21, 23
beavers 10, 140–41
Beeching, Dr Richard 131, 152,
   153

bees 229
Bekker, Hans 224, 225
Bell, Jo 124, 126–7, 131, 133,
   136–7
Belmarsh Prison, London 13
Belsey, Valerie 108–11, 114
Benn, Hilary 8, 9
biodiversity 5, 6, 51–2, 54–6, 65,
   140, 144, 168–9, 213–4,
   216, 219, 228, 230, 247
   biodiversity offsetting 172–3
'biophilia' 5
Birchover, Derbyshire 95
birds 50, 82–3, 151, 177–8, 200,
   201, 206, 208–10
   buzzards 179, 187
   dunnock 29
   fulmars 82–3
   guillemots 82
   mollymawks 82
   pigeons 183
   ptarmigan 206, 207
   starlings 210
   wagtails 202
Blackbourn, Simon 15–16, 20

Blaney, Cindy 165–7
blood sports 50
BOATs (byways open to all
    traffic) 115, 116
bog oak 65
Bookchin, Murray 239
Bridgewater Canal 128
British Hedgehog Preservation
    Society 235
Bronze Age 13, 14, 15, 17, 18,
    20, 23, 25, 77, 103
Buglife (charity) 198
butterfly, brown hairstreak 4–5,
    217
buzzards 179, 187

C
Cadbury, Helen 127, 137
Caesar, Julius 30
Cameron, David 9
Canada 206
Canal and River Trust 136, 140,
    147, 148, 240
Canal Laureate 124, 137
canals 123–49
    Ashby 146
    Bridgewater 128
    Dudley No. 2 132–3
    Grand Union 127, 129, 130,
        134, 140, 142, 186
    history 128–30
    horses 129, 143
    Inland Waterways Association
        130, 131
    invasive flora and fauna 145–8

locks 127
maintenance 139, 141–2
pollution 132–3, 144
renovation of 130–2
wildlife 135–7, 139, 140–41,
    142–3, 144, 145–7, 148
Carroll, Lewis 60
Chell, Edward 184–5
Chelmorton, Derbyshire 87
Cherwell river 124–5
Chirk, north Wales 74
cities, design of 247
Clare, John 10, 34, 42
Cocker, Mark 81
Columella 29
Combestone Tor, Dartmoor
    22–6
Commonwealth Agriculture
    Bureaux International
    147
connectivity 2, 3, 5, 6, 9, 162,
    188, 224–5, 228, 232,
    240, 241
    reconnection 242–8
Copenhagen, Denmark 182
coppicing 41, 189
Corsie, Caroline 215–19
Country Landowners' Association
    39, 40
crayfish 146
crested newts 202
Croatia 222
Cupani, Francisco 162
Cursus, Stonehenge 21
Cuthbert, Mary 96

D
Danish scurvygrass 196–7
Darlington, Mim 198
Dartmoor, Devon 14–19, 20–21,
    22–6, 99–101, 109, 150–51
  Combestone Tor 22–6
  geology 101
  Grimspound 16, 17–19
  Hay Tor 109, 150, 151
  Hookner Tor 18–19
  Legendary Dartmoor
    (website) 19
  Merrivale 20–21
  tramline 150–51
deer 178, 191, 201–2
Denmark 182
  Copenhagen 182
Derbyshire 9, 84, 85, 86, 87, 89,
    90, 95, 211
  Birchover 95–6
  Chelmorton 87
  Edensor 211
  Gardom's Edge 91
  Hartington 84, 85, 86
  Monyash 89, 90, 92
Deregulation Act (2015) 238
Devil's Punchbowl, Surrey
    243–6
Devon 14–19, 20–21, 22–5, 54,
    99–101, 108–14
  Dartmoor 14–19, 20–21,
    22–5, 99–101, 109, 150–51
  Staverton 110
Devon Hedge Group 54
Dines, Dr Trevor 196

Dingle, Rob 73–8
ditches and dykes 58–78
  etymology 60
  fens 59, 61–72
  Offa's Dyke 73–8
  wildlife 72
Domesday Book 30
dormice 193
Dorset 61, 117–21, 154
  Lyme Regis 61
  Marshwood 121
Doyle, Joe 186–90, 193–5
Dudley No. 2 Canal 132–3
dunnock 29
dykes *see* ditches and dykes

E
Edensor, Derbyshire 211
Edstone Aqueduct, 137–8
Egerton, Francis, 3rd Duke of
    Bridgewater 128
Enclosure Act (1815) 59
enclosures 10–11, 23–4, 32–5,
    43, 55, 59, 87, 224
  Enclosure Act (1815) 59
  granting of 32
Europe's Field Boundaries
    (Muller) 41
'extinction of experience' 32

F
farming 38, 40, 46–7, 49–51,
    63–4, 67, 217, 219–20, 232
fens 59, 61–72
  Great Fen Project 61–72

Feral (Monbiot) 37
fertilisers 51
Fiennes, Celia 63
flooding 58–9
foxes 206
fragmentation 3–4, 9–10, 30, 88, 121, 135, 161, 171, 173, 181, 187, 199–201, 205, 207, 221–5, 228
   fences 222
   gates 221, 222
   HS2 172, 173, 236–7
   walls 223
   see also unfragmentation
Froglife (charity) 178–9, 227
fulmars 82–3

G
Gallic Wars, The (Caesar) 30
Game and Wildlife Conservation Trust 49
Gardom's Edge, Derbyshire 91
geology of Britain 7–8
   chalk grassland 105–6
   Dartmoor 101
   Peak District 93, 101
Germany 42, 50
giant hogweed 147, 163, 183
Gielen, Jef 41
GLASS (Green Lane Association) 115–16
Glidden, Joseph 45
Glover, Ian 209, 213–14
Goddard, Jeff 116
Gould, Stephen Jay 5

Grace-Fensome, Amy 22
Graham, Tim 232
Grand Union Canal 127, 129, 130, 134, 140, 142
Great Fen Project 61–72
Great Green Wall, Africa 223, 236
Green Bridges, A Literature Review 225
'green corridors' 9
green lanes 31, 102, 107–21
   definition of 115
   GLASS (Green Lane Association) 115–16
   'green-lane effect' 113
   neglect 116, 117
   wildlife 112–14, 118
Green Lanes of England, The (Belsey) 108
Green, Duncan 115
Griffiths, Jay 28
Grimspound, Dartmoor 16, 17–19
guillemots 82

H
habitat fragmentation *see* fragmentation
Hægtesse 28–9
Harroway, The 102
Hartington, Derbyshire 84, 85, 86
hawthorn 28
Hay Tor, Dartmoor 109, 150, 151

Hedgehog Improvement Area,
    Solihull 234–5
hedgehogs 3, 4, 6, 28, 39–40,
    94, 178, 199, 227–8, 234–6
hedges 10, 28–57
    and nature conservation 52–3,
        56
    benefits of 49–51
    condition 43
    disadvantages of 49
    ecosystem 47
    etymology 28–9
    laying 35–8, 48, 216, 219
    management 35, 41, 45, 48
    origins 29–31
    trees 33, 37–8
    wildlife 33, 44, 47, 54–5,
        56–7
herbicides 51
Herefordshire 73
    Kington 73
Highgate, London 165–7
Highways England 185, 186–7,
    190, 200, 240
History of the Countryside, The
    (Rackham) 22
holly 38, 92–3
Holme Fen 62
Homo erectus 11
Hookner Tor, Dartmoor 18–19
Hooper, Dr Max 55
'Hooper's Rule' 55, 56, 113
horses 129, 177
Hosking, Rebecca 52
Hoskins, W. G. 12

HS2 172, 173, 236–7
Humberhead Levels Living
    Landscape project 231–2

I
Icknield Way, The 102
Ida of Northumbria 30
industrial agriculture 120
Industrial Revolution 11, 33, 37,
    45, 128, 153, 162
Inland Waterways Association
    131
insects 49, 220, 232
invasive flora and fauna 145–8
Iron Age 88, 175

J
Juniper, Tony 53

K
kelp 79–80
Kent 172
    Lodge Hill 172
Kington, Herefordshire 73
Krznaric, Roman 6

L
Lack, Andrew 239
'Lane, The' (Thomas) 112
Langbein, Jochen 201
Lawton, Sir John 9, 62, 168, 181,
    213–4, 228–32
leats 17
Legendary Dartmoor (website)
    19

Leiden, Netherlands 139
lichen 7, 33, 81
Line Made by Walking, A (Long)
117, 221
Linear Infrastructure Network
(LINet) 240–41
Lodge Hill, Kent 172
Long Bridges nature
reserve 123
Long, Richard 117, 221
Lons, Hermann 42
Lovejoy, David 186–90, 191,
193–5
Lyme Regis, Dorset 61

M
*Making of the British Landscape,
The* (Pryor) 7, 176–7
*Making of the English Landscape,
The* (Hoskins) 12
Making Space for Nature (White
Paper) 8, 214, 228–30
Marlborough Downs, Wiltshire
232–4
Marshwood Vale, Dorset 121
Martin, Roy 132, 133
Massaria 212
Merrivale, Dartmoor 20–21
Mesolithic period 14, 27, 91
mining 85–6, 88
mink 145–6
moles 136
mollymawks 82
Monbiot, George 37, 53, 65–6
Monyash, Derbyshire 90

Moorhouse, Tom 146
moose 206
More, Sir Thomas 33
Muller, Georg 41–2, 50, 54, 88

N
Narrow Boat (Rolt) 131, 133
National Grid 204, 209, 210,
213, 215, 217, 220, 240
National Hedge Laying
Championships 36, 48
'National Nature Network'
report 168
Natural Choice (White Paper)
237
Natural Connections (report)
238
Natural England 157, 168, 210,
225, 238, 241
'Natural Grid' 213, 218, 220,
224
nature conservation 52–3, 56
Nature Improvement Areas
(NIAs) 9, 231–4
NatureBuzz (app) 238
Navigations, The 128
Neeves, Octavia 154–65
Neolithic period 11, 13, 14, 77,
91, 92, 103, 104, 233
Netherlands 59, 139, 200, 224,
225, 226
Leiden 139
nettles 75
Network Rail 154, 159, 160, 161,
164, 240

New Networks for Nature
    conference 53
New Wild, The (Pearce) 197
Nilson, Lars 227
North Ronaldsay, Orkneys
    79–83
Norway 205–6

O
off-roading 115–17
Offa, king of Mercia 73
Offa's Dyke 73–8
'One Green Field' (Thomas) 35
ornithologists 83
Otmoor, Oxfordshire 59, 60
otters 136, 149
Oxford 124, 146
Oxford ragwort 162
Oxfordshire 59, 60
    Uffington White Horse 103
    Wayland's Smithy 104–5

P
Parma, Laurie 238
Pauly, Daniel 180
Peak District 84–99, 211
    geology 93, 101
Pearce, Fred 197
Pearce, Huma 165–7
'Penny Hedge' 31
pennywort 147
People's Trust for Endangered
    Species 180, 235
Petrovan, Silviu 227
pigeons 183

pipelines 211–12
    trees 211–12
    underground cables 211
    wildlife 212
Plantlife (charity) 196, 198
Plester, Chris 215
pollarding 41
Pontcysyllte Aqueduct, Wales 145
Pretty, Jules 238
Pryor, Francis 7, 12, 176
ptarmigan 206, 207
pylons 204–10, 212–13
    aesthetics of 210–13
    collisions 206–9
    cryptic disturbance 207
    management 214–20
    piecemeal disturbance 207
    power lines 205–10
    substations 213, 215, 216
    ultraviolet light 205–6
    underground cabling 211
    wildlife 205–10, 214–20

R
rabbits 89, 180
Rackham, Oliver 22, 31, 43, 44,
    55, 88
railways 129–30, 150–74
    building 153
    environmental management
        168–70, 189
    HS2 172, 173, 236–7
    'leaves on the line' 159–60
    maintenance 154, 159–61
    safety 170–71

railways – *Cont.*
snow 160
soft estate 154, 169, 185–6,
189
trees 154, 159–60, 169, 170
tunnels 165–7
wildlife 152–3, 156–8, 161,
162, 163, 164–5, 168–9,
171–2
Raistrick, Arthur 34
Raiter, Keren 207
Rattlechain Lagoon 132–3
reaves 13–27
Rebecca Riots 176
reindeer 205–6
Richard I, king of England 31
Ridgeway, The 102–8, 116
rights of way 115
rivers 123, 124–5, 128
Navigations, The 128
wildlife 140, 145–7
roads 175–203
anti-road protests 181, 187
construction 181
environmental management
186–90, 198–9
litter 192–3
origin 175–6
roadkill 178–81, 184, 199
soft estate 184–5, 186–95
turnpikes 176
verges 178, 195–9
wildlife 177–9, 184–5, 187,
191, 196–203
Robinson, Dr Mark 140–42, 148

Rolt, Lionel Thomas Caswall
130–31, 133, 135
Romans 24, 59, 75, 77, 175–6
RSPB 69, 240
'runrigs' 92
Ruskin, John 152
Ryme's Reedbed 71

S
Sahara Desert 223
Sandles, Tim 19
Sangwine, Tony 186–90, 193–5
sedum 100
sheep 80–2, 87, 90, 178, 199
Sheffield 172
Smithy Wood 172
Sherard, William 162
'shifting baselines' 180
Skanska 186
SLoSS (Single Large or Several
Small) 4–5
Slovenia 222
Smithy Wood, Sheffield 172
smoots 89
soft estate 154, 169, 184–5,
186–95
solar eclipse 24–5
Somerset 13
Somerset Levels 10, 59, 177
Sotherton, Nick 49–50
speed of transportation 173–4
Spelman, Caroline 237
spiders 93, 143
starlings 210
Staverton, Devon 110

Stonehenge 21–2
Stratford-upon-Avon,
    Warwickshire 130, 138
Strong, Dr Neil 168–9
Surrey 243–6
    Devil's Punchbowl 243–6
Sustrans 153
Swaledale, Yorkshire 232
'Sweet Track' 13–14

T
Tanzania 180
Telling the Bees (band) 59
terrapins 146
Thomas, Edward 35, 112
Thompson, Simon 234–5
Through the Looking-Glass (Carroll)
    60
toads 179
tramline, Dartmoor 150–51
transhumance 110
Transport for London 166
tree sparrows 233–4
treeline 10
Trends in Ecology and Evolution
    (Raiter) 207
Trump, Donald 223
Truswell, Cirhan 215
turnpikes 176
Tyler, Dr Nicholas 205–6

U
Uffington White Horse,
    Oxfordshire 103
Ullyett, Mark 62–72

unfragmentation 221–42, 245–8
    conservation corridors 223,
        229
    cost of 237–9
    road removal 226
    value of nature 230–1
    wildlife bridges 224, 225, 244
    wildlife tunnels 224–7, 235
    see also fragmentation
USA 45–6, 178, 200, 206, 208,
    226
Utopia (More) 33

V
Vermuyden, Sir Cornelius 59
voles
    bank 5
    water 136, 146, 189–90

W
wagtails 202
walkers/walking 116, 117, 134
walls 79–101
    chalk grassland 105–6
    flora 105–6
    money-safe-stones 97
    plants 99–100
    smoots 89
    stone wall styles 88–9
    through-stones 92
    wildlife 93–5
Walton, Robert 54–5
Walton Basin 77
Warwickshire Wildlife Trust 234
water voles 136, 146, 189–90

Wayland's Smithy, Oxfordshire
104–5
Wells, William 69
wetlands 58–9, 62, 226, 231–2
Whitby, Yorkshire 31
White, Nicholas 241, 242
Whittlesea Mere 63, 69
Wilde, Oscar 239
Wilson, E. O. 5
Wiltshire 20, 102, 232–4
Marlborough Downs 232–4
Stonehenge 21–2

wind turbines 81, 213
Woodwalton Fen 62
Worcestershire Wildlife Trust
214–5
Wragg, Trevor 84–99

Y
Yorkshire 231–232
Swaledale 232
Whitby 31
Yorkshire Dales National Park
232